COTSWO

C000319249

Teashop Walks

Jean Patefield

COUNTRYSIDE BOOKS

NEWBURY, BERKSHIRE

First published 1996
© Jean Patefield 1996

Revised and updated 2002

All rights reserved. No reproduction
permitted without the prior permission
of the publisher:

COUNTRYSIDE BOOKS
3 Catherine Road
Newbury, Berkshire

ISBN 1 85306 390 8

Designed by Mon Mohan
Cover illustration by Colin Doggett
Photographs and maps by the author

Produced through MRM Associates Ltd., Reading
Printed by J. W. Arrowsmith Ltd., Bristol

Contents

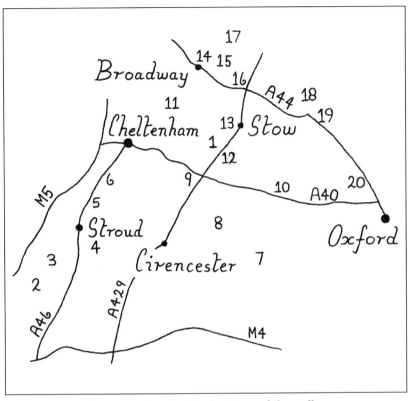

Area map showing the locations of the walks.

Key to route maps

Route	– – →–	Teashop	☕
Other paths and tracks	⋯	Pub referred to in text	PH
Road	═══		
Railway	++++++	Summit	△
River	∿∿∿	Point in text	⑤
Lake	⬭	Car park	▫
Church	†	Building referred to in text	◼

Introduction

Anyone in search of the true English countryside need look no further than the Cotswolds, considered by many to be among the most beautiful areas in England and certainly the most typically English. The Cotswolds are limestone and this has a profound effect on both countryside and town, uniting landscape and architecture into one unique whole. The limestone mass has been lifted and tilted by geological forces so there is the steep scarp slope of the Cotswold Edge to the west and the long dip slope to the east.

The walks in this book are all between 2^1/$_2$ and 6 miles and should be within the capacity of the average person, including those of mature years and families with children. They are intended to take the walker through some of the most attractive scenery and loveliest towns and villages in Central England at a gentle pace with plenty of time to stop and stare, to savour the beauty and interest all around. A dedicated yomper could probably knock off the whole book in a single weekend but in doing so they would have missed the point and seen nothing. To appreciate the countryside fully it is necessary to go slowly with your eyes and ears open.

The Cotswolds, now designated an Area of Outstanding Natural Beauty, are about people and buildings and differ in this respect from other tourist areas, notably the wilder and mountainous National Parks of the north and west. Some of the Cotswolds' sons and daughters have been important and famous people; others are just as interesting but more obscure. Such a long history has left its mark on the countryside and the buildings so there is much that is fascinating to see and this can add enormously to the pleasure of a walk. Therefore, as well as giving instructions for the route itself, I have also included information about the interesting features to be seen on the way.

Some of the walks involve a little climbing. This is inevitable as hills add variety to the countryside and much of the Cotswolds is so attractive because of its rolling character. However, this presents no problem to the sensible walker who has three uphill gears - slowly, very slowly and admiring the view. None of the walks in this book are inherently hazardous but sensible care should be taken. A lot of the falls that do happen are due to unsuitable footwear, particularly unridged soles since grass slopes can be as slippery as the more obviously hazardous wet, smooth rock. Proper walking shoes or boots also give some protection to the ankle. It is, of course, essential to watch where you place your feet to avoid tripping up. Wainwright, the doyen of walkers in the Lake District, said that he never had a serious fall in all his years and thousands of miles of walking because he always looked where he put his feet and stopped if he wanted to admire the scenery.

All the routes are on public rights of way or permissive paths and have been carefully checked, but things do change in the countryside; a gate is replaced by a stile or a wood is extended. Each walk is circular and is illustrated by a sketch map. An Ordnance Survey sheet is useful as well, especially for identifying the main features of views. There are several from which to choose. The area is covered by Landranger 1:50 000 (1¼ inches to 1 mile) series sheets 150, 151, 162, 163, 164 and 173. The Ordnance Survey also produces a 1 inch to 1 mile Touring Map and Guide which is very useful. In addition there are the Pathfinder 1:25 000 maps, each of which covers a smaller area at a larger scale. The grid reference of the starting point and the appropriate Landranger map are given for each walk.

The walks are designed so that, starting where suggested, the teashop is reached in the second half, so a really good appetite for tea can be worked up and then its effects walked off. Some walks begin at a car park, which is ideal. Where this is not possible, the recommended starting place will always have somewhere where a few cars can be left without endangering other traffic. However, it sometimes fits in better with the plans for the day to start and finish at the teashop and so for each walk there are details of how to do this.

Tea is often said to be the best meal to eat out in England and I believe that it is something to be enjoyed on all possible occasions. Scones with cream and strawberry jam, delicious home-made cakes, toasted teacakes dripping with butter in winter, delicate cucumber sandwiches in summer, all washed down with the cup that cheers! Bad for the figure maybe, but the walking will see to that.

The best teashops offer a range of cakes, all home-made and including fruit cake, as well as scones and other temptations. Cream teas should, of course, feature clotted cream. Teapots should be capacious and pour properly. Most of the teashops visited on these walks fulfil all these criteria admirably and they all provide a good tea. They always serve at least light lunches as well so there is no need to think of these walks as just something for the afternoons.

The pleasures of summer walking are obvious. Most of the teashops featured in this book have an attractive garden where tea can be taken outside when the weather is suitable. However, let me urge you not to overlook the pleasures of a good walk in winter. The roads and paths are quieter and what could be better than sitting by an open fire in a cosy teashop scoffing crumpets that you can enjoy with a clear conscience due to the brisk walk to get them!

Teashops are not scattered evenly throughout the Cotswolds. In some places popular with tourists, the visitor is spoilt for choice. In such cases the teashop that, in the author's opinion, most closely fulfils the criteria set out above is recommended but should that not appeal, there are others from which to choose. Sometimes there is a delightful walk to be enjoyed but the choice for tea is more limited, so a few of the teashops visited on the circuits in this book are in unusual places such as gardens and stately homes. However, that in itself adds interest to the route and they all offer an excellent tea partway round an attractive walk.

The opening times and telephone number of each teashop are given. Some are rather vague about when they open out of season – it seems to depend on weather and mood. If you are planning a walk on a wet November Tuesday, for example, a call to check that tea will actually be available that day is a wise precaution. A few are definitely closed in the depths of winter and for these walks an alternative source of refreshment is given. In most cases, these are pubs serving food which in some cases includes tea.

So put on your walking shoes and prepare to be delighted, by the Cotswold scenery and a traditional English cream tea!

Jean Patefield
Spring 1996

1

THE SLAUGHTERS AND THE WINDRUSH VALLEY

This particularly fine walk encapsulates all that is best about the Cotswolds. It explores two exceptionally pretty villages, one where an old mill has been converted into a craft shop and tea room. The route wends its way by paths, tracks and lanes through some fine scenery with excellent views and passes the site of a third village, now lost but not forgotten, as it has been the site of a modern controversy. All in all, a highly recommended walk that is just as good in winter as in summer.
Distance: 5¹/₂ miles.

The Old Mill in Lower Slaughter is unusually built of brick when all around is local stone. The building has been restored as a tearoom, craft shop and museum. The menu is limited to delicious cakes or organic ice cream, which you may taste free, so other arrangements are needed for lunch. It is open every day between 10 am and 6 pm from 1st March until the clocks go back in the autumn. In winter it closes at dusk, but it is a good idea to call to check. Telephone: 01451 820052.

Starting point: The Square, Upper Slaughter (GR 155231).

How to get there: From the B4068 Stow-on-the-Wold Cheltenham road at Lower Swell one mile west of Stow, take a minor road signed 'The Slaughters'. Bear right at a fork after ¼ mile and continue to Upper Slaughter. There is some parking on the left as you enter the village or in The Square on the right.

Map: OS Outdoor Leisure 45 The Cotswolds.

Alternative starting point: If you wish to visit the teashop at the beginning or end of your walk, start in Lower Slaughter where there is some street parking (see walk 12). The teashop is in the Mill, signed in the village. You will then start the walk at point 8.

The Walk

One rector of the much-restored Norman church was Reverend F. E. Witts, whose Diary of a Cotswold Parson *is an entertaining picture of Cotswold life. He must have been well-liked in his day as the imposing tomb in the church was paid for by public subscription. He was also lord of the manor, and the former rectory is now the Lords of the Manor Hotel. The older Manor House is claimed by many to be the finest house of its period in the Cotswolds. It is not open to the public. The attractive cottages round The Square were remodelled by the famous architect Edwin Lutyens.*

1. With your back to the church turn right to continue on the lane out of the village. At a T-junction continue ahead on a sunken path. Near the top of the hill, go through a gate on the right then go ahead to pick up a grassy track that leads to a second gate and on through a third gate to emerge on a minor road.

2. Cross the road to press on in the same direction along a lane signed 'Lower Harford 1'.

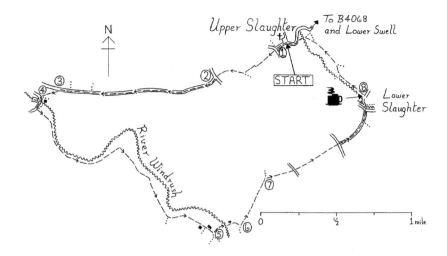

3. After about a mile take a signed path on the left leading diagonally down across a field towards a farm seen below. Go through a metal kissing gate and down some steps onto a lane.

This is the site of the medieval village of Lower Harford. Like many other communities it dwindled under the combined pressures of the Black Death and changes in farming. It has been the site of a modern local controversy. It was proposed to close a path through the farm, not shown on the OS Leisure Map. This was opposed by the Open Spaces Society on the grounds of the historic importance of the path, which has been in use from at least AD 743 when it was known as Mylew Weg or Mill Lane. They won the appeal and this is the reason for the notices suggesting an alternative route, used on this walk.

4. Turn left and cross a ford using a footbridge. Some 150 yards after the ford turn left on a bridleway, signed 'Windrush Way'. Follow the clear, way-marked path for 1½ miles, passing through woods, across a field and between farm buildings to emerge on a lane that is scarcely more than a track.

5. Turn left, again signed 'Windrush Way'. Cross the stream and pass in front of an attractive old house.

11

6. At a T-Junction with a cross track turn left, now signed 'Gloucestershire Way'. Walk up the track and go through a gate into a field. Continue in the same direction along the right hand side of the field and for 70 yards along the right hand side of a second field.

7. Turn right on a signed path across a field to a lane. Cross the lane and continue in the same direction on a fenced path to a second lane. Keep going in the same direction now on a lane into Lower Slaughter. At a T-junction go over a footbridge slightly to the left. Turn left on the far side and follow the footway round to the teashop in an old mill building.

Some prefer the more manicured charms of Lower Slaughter where it has been said, truthfully, that even the council houses have roofs of local stone. Others favour Upper Slaughter but it has to be admitted that they are both exceptionally attractive. The rather gruesome names of the villages have nothing to do with battles or massacres — see Walk 12.

8. Turn left out of the teashop and almost immediately left again, signed 'Warden's Way'. When the path forks bear right through a metal kissing gate and walk across three fields to a small gate giving onto a footbridge over a river. Now follow the clear path ahead to a road. Turn left back to the start.

2

WOTTON-UNDER-EDGE

This varied, interesting circuit starts with a short climb and I think you will agree that it is well worth the modest effort when you see the splendid views to be enjoyed. The walk visits two vantage points on the south-western edge of the Cotswolds and has a short and easy optional extension to a third with interesting historical associations. The route then drops down to the friendly town of Wotton-under-Edge for tea and it is worth taking some time to explore this fascinating and ancient place. A level stroll by a stream returns you to the start.
Distance: 5 miles (plus a possible ¹/₂ mile extension).

Wotton Coffee Shop (also a guest house) is on the Cotswold Way, which runs through Wotton-under-Edge, and positively welcomes walkers. The range of cakes offered is very tempting and there are cream teas and lots of other goodies. Light

lunches are served, including filled jacket potatoes, as well as more substantial meals such as curries and casseroles. At the back is a beautiful walled garden. It is open every day except Sunday, from 9 am to 5 pm throughout the year.
Telephone: 01453 843158.

Starting point: Coombe pumping station (GR 767938).

How to get there: From the B4058 Wotton-under-Edge to Nailsworth road ½ mile north-east of Wotton-under-Edge, take a minor road signed 'Coombe'. Follow this right down through the village to the bottom of the hill. There are several spots just by the pumping station where it is possible to park without causing inconvenience.

Map: OS Landranger 162 Gloucester and Forest of Dean.

Alternative starting point: If you want to visit the teashop at the beginning or end of your walk, start in Wotton-under-Edge, where there is ample parking in the town car park, just behind the High Street. The teashop is on the High Street, almost opposite the Co-op. You will then start the walk at point 11.

The Walk

1. From Coombe pumping station take the lane to the right of Chestnut Cottage. Turn right at the first junction and left at the second to zigzag up the hill. Stay on this very quiet lane to the junction with the main road.

2. Take a footpath directly opposite the junction. Near the top of the hill cross a stile on the left and follow the path along the top of a field.

3. When the hedge on the right turns right at a corner go over a stile by a gate on the right onto a track. As the track bends right take a path on the left and then bear right when the path forks after 20 yards to walk, with a fence on the right, to a lane.

4. Take a bridleway along a track 30 yards to the left and continue, with a wood on the right and a hedge on the left. When the track swings right into the wood, go ahead on a path.

5. As the wood starts on the left, there is a very complex junction of paths. Think of it like a roundabout and take the third exit, which is almost straight ahead, slightly right. Bear left when the path forks after

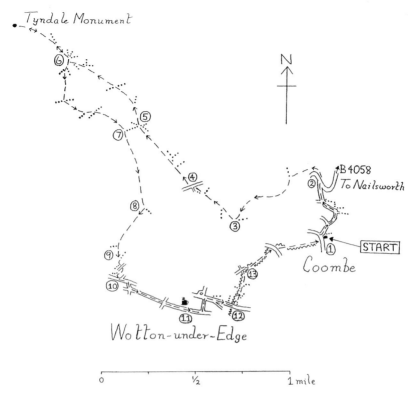

Tyndale Monument

N

⑥

⑤

⑦

④

B 4058
② To Nailsworth

⑧

③

START
①

⑨

⑬

Coombe

⑩

⑪

⑫

Wotton-under-Edge

0   ½   1 mile

200 yards. Go straight across a wide track and stay on this path, ignoring paths on the right and left, to a T-junction with a cross-path.

To visit the Tyndale Monument on Nibley Knoll. This is a short extension of about ¹/₄ mile each way and is strongly recommended for its fine views:

a) Turn right and when the path forks after 25 yards bear left on the main path, marked by blue arrows.

b) Follow this path through the woods and the monument comes into view.

c) Follow the path by the fence to the monument.

d) After admiring the view and identifying the features shown on the topograph, retrace your steps to the junction.

15

The Tyndale Monument was erected in the 19th century in memory of William Tyndale, who was born near here. The monument is locked and the key is available in North Nibley at the bottom of the hill (not visited on this walk). William Tyndale had left the area by the time he translated the Bible into English, the activity which led to his being strangled and burned at the stake in 1536.

6. Turn left (straight on if you have been to the monument). Almost immediately the path forks. Bear right then turn left after 30 yards. The path is indicated by a Cotswold Way sign, marked with a yellow arrow and white dot. Continue over a cross-path. When another path joins on the right, stay on the main path as it bends left. A second path joins on the right and after 10 yards you fork right.

7. At a T-junction with a cross-path turn right and follow the path along the edge of the wood.

8. When the wood on the right ends, by a National Trust sign for Westridge Wood, turn right to walk along the right-hand side of a field with the wood on the right. Cross the stile at the far end of the field and bear left to a walled enclosure. Here the views are once again magnificent and there are several welcome seats from which to admire them.

The original trees were planted to mark the victory at Waterloo. They were felled and used in a bonfire to celebrate the end of the Crimean War and then the wall was built and more trees planted to celebrate Queen Victoria's Jubilee in 1887. More trees were added in 1952.

9. Take a path steeply downhill from the enclosure towards Wotton-under-Edge directly below. Continue on the path across a lane, and by houses carry on downhill to a road.

10. Turn left. Pass by Old London Road. Turn right at the next junction and follow this road into the town centre, crossing Bear Street at its junction with Haw Street. The teashop is on the left, about two-thirds of the way along, almost opposite the Co-op.

Wotton's full name clearly describes its position under the Cotswold escarpment. It has had a long and fascinating history, which has left its legacy in the many interesting buildings. The Historical Society runs a Heritage Centre, housing displays about the town's varied past. This is located in a converted fire station, overlooking the car park reached if you turn right down Market Street, off the High Street. It is open from Tuesday to Saturday, 10 am to 5 pm in the summer and 10 am to 4 pm in the winter, also on the first Sunday of the month between June and October (telephone: 01453 521541). Here you will find more information and leaflets about all there is to be seen, and a visit followed by a walk about the town is highly recommended if you have time.

Some memorable characters have been associated with Wotton-under-Edge. The town's early history was tied up with the Berkeley family who owned the local manor. Thomas, Lord Berkeley, was an exceptional man. He fought the Scots for Richard II, then for Henry IV he was Admiral of the fleet that defeated the French at Milford Haven – and he was with Henry V at Agincourt. He was devoted to his wife Margaret and did not remarry when she died young, leaving just a daughter who eventually married the Earl of Warwick. The lack of a male heir ultimately led to a dispute over the titles and property, which resulted in a full scale battle between private armies in which several hundred men were killed. This was the last battle between private armies on English soil and took place at North Nibley. Thomas died in 1417 and there are magnificent brasses of him and his wife Margaret in the parish church. The originals are kept safe and fibre-glass replicas are on public view. Another man with associations with Wotton who has made his mark on the world and is, perhaps, better remembered is Sir Isaac Pitman, who invented modern shorthand while teaching in the town.

11. From the teashop turn left along the High Street, then left along Church Street. At the next junction turn right and follow the road to the bottom of the dip.

12. Some 15 yards after crossing the stream turn left along an alley between houses. At a T-junction with a cross-path turn left and follow the path beside the stream to the second footbridge.

13. Over the bridge turn right to continue by the stream on a surfaced path crossing and recrossing the stream. Turn right at a lane and left after 20 yards to continue by the stream back to the start.

3

ULEY and OWLPEN

This is a short but energetic walk with a steep climb near the start to the Iron Age fort at Uley Bury. However, don't let that put you off as the views are truly superb, perhaps the best from any route in this book. Also, you will be rewarded with an outstanding tea, so the effort is well worth while. Distance: 3^1/$_2$ miles.

The Cyder House Restaurant at Owlpen Manor is situated in a 15th-century building with cruck trusses and a huge oak cider press dating from 300 years ago when cider feasts were held here. Delicous cakes and puddings are served, as well as cream teas and lunches (though the latter might be a little formal for a walk). It is open every day except Monday (open Bank Holiday Mondays) from the beginning of April until the end of September between 12.30 pm and 5 pm.

Telephone: 01453 860261.

This outstanding walk demanded to be included even though the opening hours of the teashop, which is highly recommended, are rather restricted. If you decide to enjoy it when the teashop is closed, an alternative source of refreshment is the Old Crown Inn in Uley, passed very close to the end of the walk, a free house serving bar meals.

Starting point: The directions for this walk start from Uley church (GR 791986).

How to get there: Uley is on the B4066 Dursley to Stroud road. There is no public car park but there are several spots where it is possible to leave a car without causing inconvenience to others.

Map: OS Landranger 162 Gloucester and Forest of Dean.

Alternative starting point: If you want to visit the teashop at the beginning or end of the walk, start at Owlpen, where there is a car park. You would now commence at point 10.

The Walk

Uley was a prosperous wool town in the 18th century. Stroud clad the British army in scarlet, but Uley blue was almost as famous. As well as 18 mills, there were 11 ale houses which Samuel Rudder, a local commentator of the time, blamed for much of the 'idleness and debauchery' he found in Uley. The handloom weavers, on whose labour this prosperity was built, had a hard life and their pay was pitiful. They formed societies, the forerunners of trade unions, which had to be secret because they were illegal. After strikes and riots their conditions gradually improved. Many of the fine houses that grace Uley date from this time so the prosperity of the mill owners was obviously not too seriously affected. After 1810 the wool industry moved elsewhere and the local economy was severely depressed as mills closed.

The handsome Victorian church was designed by S.S. Teulon, who was also responsible for the Tyndale Monument visited on walk 2. This is the third church to be built on the site and it dates from 1857, a time when there was great enthusiasm for modernising or replacing old churches.

1. Take the path signed 'Uley Bury and Whitecourt' to the right of the church, opposite Green Close. Stay on the path by the church wall, ignoring a path on the right.

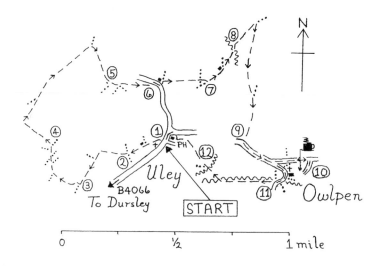

2. Cross a track and continue in the same direction, passing through a wooden kissing-gate. After another gate the path is fenced. Follow this until it ends at a stile by a gate and then continue ahead along the left-hand side of a field.

3. Turn right at a surfaced track, signed 'Uley Bury'. At Whitecourt waterworks leave the surfaced track and continue by the fence to a stile and gate into a wood. Bear right on a path, steeply up through the wood onto a mound, ignoring paths to the right and left.

4. At the top bear left and follow the path round for 3/4 mile, crossing a track.

Uley Bury is an Iron Age hill fort built on a promontory of the escarpment and so commanding wide views over the surrounding country. It encloses about 30 acres and could have given shelter to some 2,000 people when danger threatened. It has not been fully excavated but chance finds, kept in Gloucester and Stroud museums, include material from the 1st to the 4th century AD, as well as Iron Age pottery and coins, showing that the site was occupied in Roman times.

5. Watch for a signed bridleway on the left going steeply downhill. Take this and at a cross-path in front of a gate and stile, turn left to eventually reach a road.

6. Turn right along the road for 200 yards. Immediately after Crawley House turn left on a track. After 20 yards turn right over a stile. DO NOT go in the direction shown by the arrow on the stile but head along the right-hand side of the field in the direction of a barn to a stile where the hedge on the right ends and a fence starts.

7. Turn left along a track, keeping the barn on the left. Just 10 yards after a gate across the track bear half-right across a field. At the time of writing the path was not visible on the ground. Cross a stream at a culvert and cut half-left across the corner of the next field to a stile.

8. The right of way lies diagonally right towards a gate in the top right corner of the field and then doubles back on a clear track along the top of the field. Follow the track to a lane.

9. Turn left, then go left again on a track to the manor, following it round past the car park to the restaurant.

'Owlpen in Gloucestershire – ah, what a dream is there!' said Vita Sackville-West and many, including Prince Charles, have thought it 'the epitome of the English village'. It is based round a fine 15th-century manor house, nestling in a deep, wooded valley, which grew and developed until the early 18th century. The formal terraced garden with its clipped yews is said to be the oldest complete garden in the country.

The only building dating from after the Industrial Revolution is the church, which was largely reconstructed in 1828/9 and is richly decorated with painted ceilings, mosaics and stained glass. It contains eight Daunt family brasses taken from the old church.

10. After tea return to the lane and turn left to continue along it. Some 40 yards after a right-hand bend and the postbox, cross a stile next to a field gate on the right. (There is a path which cuts across the corner to this point, but the bottom of the field can be extremely boggy so it is better to go round on the road.)

11. Walk by the stream and then cross it immediately after a large pond on the right. Head diagonally left across the field to a stile.

12. Over the stile, take the right of two faint paths, bearing just to the right of the church spire, seen up ahead. This leads to a stile onto a hedged path which leads eventually to a road. Turn left and left again, back to the church.

4

MINCHINHAMPTON

The first few yards of the walk give a misleading impression since they are uphill! After that the path levels out and this delightful short walk involves no more climbing. The route to the charming old town of Minchinhampton lies along the edge of the Golden Valley. In summer, with the trees in full leaf, the views are only periodically glimpsed. In winter when the trees are bare they are more frequent. The return is even easier, joining the outward route just before the end.
Distance: 2¹/₂ miles.

The Coffee Bean is a traditional teashop and very popular locally, especially for lunch, when it is wise to book. Full lunches are served, the menu varying from day to day, as well as soup, sandwiches and jacket potatoes – all delicious and home-made. It has an excellent selection of cakes displayed on a trolley. One speciality of the house is 'goo' which is a mouth-watering variety of caramel shortcake. The shop is open all year every day except Monday, between 9.30 am and 4 pm. On Sunday they open only for full lunches. Telephone: 01453 883382.

When the teashop is closed, there are several pubs in Minchinhampton, most notably the Crown, which has a pleasant garden.

Starting point: The National Trust sign for Hyde Common (GR 885017).

How to get there: From the A419 Stroud to Cirencester road at Chalford, 4 miles from Stroud, take a minor road signed 'Hyde 1 Minchinhampton 2'. After ³/₄ mile turn left at a round house. Turn right along Knapps Lane and park after a few yards. There is a wide verge opposite a house called Badgers Bank and several other spots where a car can be left without causing a nuisance.

Map: OS Landranger 162 Gloucester and Forest of Dean.

Alternative starting point: If you want to visit the teashop at the beginning or end of the walk, start in Minchinhampton, parking in the town. The Coffee Bean is on the High Street. You would commence at point 5.

The Walk

1. Take a path uphill by the National Trust sign for Hyde Common, opposite a lane downhill. Cross a stone stile at the path junction and continue in more or less the same direction along the top of a wood.

2. Cross a lane and continue in the same direction, ignoring a cross-path.

3. At the next lane turn left for 35 yards then cross a stone stile on the left. Head half-right across a field to a stile and then follow the path between a hedge and a wall to a lane.

4. Turn left. Cross the main road at a T-junction and take a path across the common towards the distinctive tower of Minchinhampton church. Turn right down the lane by the church and left at the junction. At the main street turn right and the teashop is about halfway down on the right.

Minchinhampton means 'nuns' place'. The parish was given by Queen

23

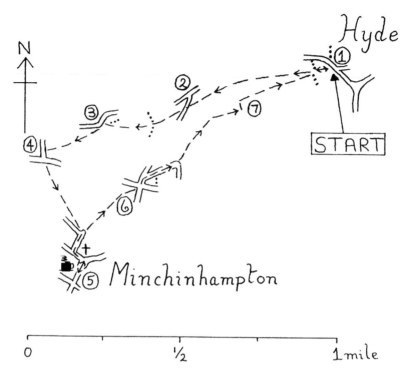

Matilda, the wife of William the Conqueror, to the Convent of the Holy Trinity of Caen in Normandy and later the nuns of Syon Abbey in Middlesex became the lords of the manor. The church has an outstanding series of brasses. The Hampton brass shows John Hampton and his wife in funeral shrouds with nine children below. Their eldest daughter was Dame Alice, shown in a nun's habit though she was not a professed nun. She was a great benefactor of Syon Abbey.

Until the Stroud to Cirencester road opened in the 19th century, Minchinhampton was a busy market town at the junction of several routes, and an important focus for the local wool trade. Sheep were grazed on the surrounding common and the wool dispatched to the mills in the valleys below. The town is centred on the attractive market square with its pillared market hall built in 1698.

5. After tea, retrace your steps up by the church. At the edge of the

common bear slightly right along its edge with a wall on the right.

Minchinhampton Common, owned by the National Trust, lies mainly to the west of the town. It is a high, grassy plateau between the deep Frome and Nailsworth valleys and has many Iron Age earthworks and a 20th-century golf course. In 1743 a crowd of 20,000 gathered on the common to hear the non-conformist preacher George Whitefield. He didn't meet with universal approval, however, as he had been beaten up in Minchinhampton a few hours earlier.

6. When the wall ends bear right to a road junction and then turn left on a minor road called The Knapp. After 30 yards turn right. When the road ends continue ahead on a track, bearing slightly left.

7. The walled track ends at a stone stile. Over the stile the path is not readily apparent on the ground. It lies to the right along the top of the field and then bears left down to a stile about two-thirds of the way along the fence. It then continues diagonally down to rejoin the outward path and thence back to the start.

5

PAINSWICK

This is a very varied walk which explores the delightful valley north of Painswick before climbing to the 'Queen of the Cotswolds' for tea. The return is over Painswick Beacon with magnificent views in all directions. Distance: 6 miles.

Chancellor's Tea Rooms in Victoria Street, Painswick offer a tempting selection, including toasted teacakes with cinnamon butter and a Special Afternoon Tea with sandwiches and scones. A variety of hot dishes, among them a vegetarian option, is served at lunchtime as well as sandwiches and home-made soup. There are two rooms, one for smokers and one with no smoking. The teashop is open from 10 am until 5.30 pm every day except Monday throughout the year. Walkers are welcome but are asked to remove muddy boots.

Telephone: 01452 812451.

Starting point: Cranham Corner (GR 881129).

How to get there: From the A46 Stroud to Cheltenham road at Cranham Corner, 2 miles south of Brockworth, take a minor road signed 'Upton St Leonards'. There is a parking space for a few cars about 50 yards along on the left by the Cotswold Way signs.

Map: OS Landranger 162 Gloucester and Forest of Dean.

Alternative starting point: If you want to visit the teashop at the beginning or end of the walk, start in Painswick, where there is ample parking in the town car park on the main road. Chancellor's Tea Rooms are on Victoria Street, near the church. You would now start the walk at point 10.

The Walk

1. Cross the lane and take the path signed 'Cotswold Way', opposite the parking place. Follow the path through the wood to the road, ignoring a path on the left through a gap in the wall.

2. Cross the main road and take the side road signed 'Cranham' and 'Birdlip'. After 100 yards turn right on a road with the sign 'Cranham 1' and 'Scout HQ'.

3. After 200 yards take a public footpath on the right between two houses, Chandos and Millfield Corner. Follow the path between hedges for a short distance and then cross a stile into a field. The path is not visible on the ground but goes along the right-hand side of the field to a stile by a gate. Immediately climb a less than obvious stile on the right and follow the path between a hedge and a fence to a house and lane.

4. Cross the lane and continue ahead through a metal gate. Take the path to pass in front of a house, seen below. The route is not always clear on the ground but follows the line of some power poles, passing another house on the right, to a lane.

5. Turn left. After 100 yards, just after a left-hand bend, go over a rickety wooden stile on the right into a field. The path is not visible on the ground now for a while. However, go forward downhill then veer right to a section of wooden fence in the hedge. Cross this and then

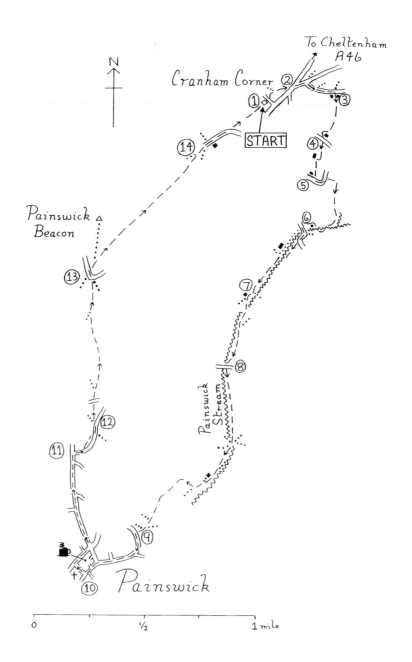

To Cheltenham
A46

Cranham Corner ②

①

③

START

⑭

④

⑤

Painswick △
Beacon

⑥

⑬

⑦

⑧

Painswick Stream

⑫

⑪

⑨

⑩ Painswick

0   ½   1 mile

bear left downhill to a stream in the valley bottom. Turn right to walk with the stream on the left and watch for a stile in the fence on the stream bank. Cross this and go ahead over a footbridge. The stream is on the right and a mill pond on the left. Some 17 yards after the footbridge turn right to recross the stream at a second footbridge. Turn left to a lane, passing a house on the left.

6. Turn left and follow the lane round a right-hand bend. In about 50 yards, as the lane bends left, cross a stile on the right to follow the stream again, now on the right. Just after a magnificent house on the right, cross the stream at a substantial footbridge and go over a stile to continue in the same direction, with the stream now on the left.

The stream the walk follows in this section is Painswick Stream. It was the source of Painswick's wealth, powering the many mills that stood on its banks.

7. Climb a stile at the end of the field and bear right, passing a house on the right. Shortly after the house turn left to follow a path through woods to a stile and then across three fields. The stream is now on the right.

8. Cross the lane and take the path directly opposite, still following the stream on the right, to a muddy track with a post festooned with blue and yellow arrows. This signifies a complex junction of paths and bridleways. Turn right, crossing the stream and, when the path shortly forks, bear left along the left-hand side of a field. Go through two gates close together and continue ahead, with a hedge on the right, to a house. Go through a gate across the path and ahead to join the track from a house. Walk along the track, ignoring a path on the left, climbing out of the valley.

9. At the road turn left and follow it round into Painswick. Keep ahead, towards the church, and the teashop is on the right.

Lovely Painswick is a feast of vernacular architecture and will repay exploring. It has a long and interesting history and was at the peak of its wealth between the 14th and 18th centuries as a wool town. This is reflected in the fine houses and the church. In the churchyard is an unrivalled collection of table and pedestal tombs. Brass plates on many of them are engraved with the names of their occupants – Lovedays, Pooles and Packers – families of rich wool merchants and clothiers. Guide books are available in the church.

The churchyard is best known, however, for its yews. Legend says that no more than 99 can be grown – if a 100th is planted it promptly dies! They are clipped into precise shapes and some have merged together to form arches across the paths. Every year, on the first Sunday after 18 September, the annual clipping ceremony takes place. The children of the village hold hands to encircle the church and dance round it, singing hymns. Afterwards, they are rewarded with a Painswick bun and a silver coin. The ceremony has nothing to do with shearing sheep but refers to the yews and was once reputedly an ale-swilling dance that has become tamed by the passing years. Over the wall of the churchyard are the stocks, introduced in the 19th century for the punishment of those 'who carry on carousels to the annoyance of their neighbours'.

Painswick was visited by Henry VIII and Anne Boleyn for a few days' holiday. The lord of the manor at the time was Sir Anthony Kingston who was a friend of the king and famous (or infamous) for his callous cruelty and willingness to carry out the monarch's dirty work. He officiated at the burning of Bishop Hooper in Gloucester. In Painswick he had a gallows permanently erected and men paid to be ready to put it to instant use. He was hated in the town and when the church was knocked about in the Civil War, the locals used it as cover to vandalise his grave. His father was Anne Boleyn's jailer and led her out to her execution.

Most of the buildings, including the modern ones, are of Cotswold stone, which contributes to the sense of place. The superb half-timbered building on the main street that this walk passes is now the post office. If you look up, there is a fire insurance plaque on it. In the 18th century the importance of Painswick drained away as the wool trade transferred to the industrial scale mills elsewhere. The small family concerns were slow to introduce the new technology, which was often opposed by the workers and so could not compete. As the mill owners tried to maintain their profits by driving down wages and employing children the poverty was terrible, leading to riots and strikes and many families leaving the area.

10. From the teashop turn right, passing the church on the left. At the main road go right and then turn left at the B4073, signed 'Gloucester'. Continue ahead at the end on the one-way system.

A little way further on along the Gloucester road is Painswick Rococo Garden. The rococo was a style briefly popular in the transition from the stylised formality of the 17th century to the more naturalistic approach to garden design of the 18th century. The Painswick garden is the only complete survivor of that period and is being restored to its original form, known because it was depicted in a contemporary painting by Thomas Robins dated 1748. This could be an alternative tea stop as teas are served in the Coach House Restaurant, open 11 am to 5 pm on Wednesday to Sunday from the beginning of February to mid-December (telephone: 01452 813204).

11. Turn right on Golf Course Road, signed 'Cemetery' and 'Cotswold Way'. Just before the road bends left take a track on the left. This rejoins the road further on, cutting off the corner. Turn left along the road for 50 yards.

12. Take a path on the left signed 'Painswick Beacon'. When it forks after 15 yards bear right on a path with the Cotswold Way logo, marked with yellow arrows and a white dot. This goes across the golf course and is, on the whole, well marked with the yellow arrow and white dot sign on posts and trees. Cross a small lane and bear right to stay close to the wall on the right. Cross another fairway and follow the path through a wood to a track. Turn right, passing a quarry filled with architectural salvage, to a road.

13. Turn left along the road and then right on a path signed 'Cotswold Way', which is easy to follow across the golf course, but does not go to the top of Painswick Beacon. This is well worth the diversion and few feet extra ascent. To go to the top of the beacon bear left at the 13th tee; to follow the main path, bear right.

Painswick Beacon has magnificent 360° views. It is topped by an Iron Age hill fort whose ramparts can still be seen. Where golfers now practise their shots, Iron Age people herded their livestock. This area is easily accessible from the road and is very popular so it can be busy on a sunny Sunday afternoon, in complete contrast to the start of the walk which is so quiet. However, few people go very far from their cars and so the crowds are soon left behind.

14. At the end of the golf course, follow a track ahead. This soon becomes a surfaced lane passing a large modern house on the right. When the lane bends right, continue ahead on a path into Buckholt Wood, signed 'Cotswold Way'. This leads back to the starting point.

Buckholt Wood is a National Nature Reserve. Its importance stems from the fact that it is a very ancient woodland with a wide variety of species. A superb example of limestone beech wood, perhaps seen at its best in autumn. Its name comes from the Saxon for beech wood. In the 12th century it was a hunting preserve of the monks of Gloucester Abbey.

6

CRANHAM and COOPER'S HILL

This must be one of the outstanding walks of the Cotswolds. Much of the route is through some of the finest and most extensive woodland in the area. It leads gently up to Cooper's Hill, famous for its cheese rolling ceremony, from which the views are stunning. After tea, the return lies through more superb woodland and passes by the site of a Roman villa. The Romans certainly knew how to pick their spot and this is tucked into the south-west face of the escarpment with lovely views. It is easy to be tempted to linger here. Distance: 3 miles.

The Haven Tea Garden at Cooper's Hill occurs at just the right place. Walkers are welcome and there is a fascinating visitors' book. Cakes and delicious sandwiches are served in the garden, which is positioned to enjoy similar views to those of the villa. Toffee made to

the recipe of a lady who used to live in the bungalow over 150 years ago is also on offer. Lunches and teas are served every day from a week before Easter to the end of October.
Telephone: 01452 863213.

When the teashop is closed, refreshment is available at the Black Horse in Cranham. From the post office turn left along the road through Cranham and then right to the pub.

Starting point: Cranham post office, adjacent to the county scout centre (GR 895131).

How to get there: Take the A46 Stroud to Cheltenham road. At Cranham Corner, 3 miles north of Painswick, take the road signed 'Cranham 1 Birdlip 3'. After 100 yards fork right for Cranham. On entering the village take a track on the left to the scout centre and post office.

Map: OS Landranger 163 Cheltenham and Cirencester.

Alternative starting point: If you want to visit the teashop at the beginning or end of the walk, start at Cooper's Hill, where there is a small car park. This is reached by turning off the A46 along a narrow lane signed 'Cooper's Hill'. You would now start the walk at point 6.

The Walk

The woods around Cranham are some of the finest and most extensive woodland in Britain. They include Buckholt Wood (see Walk 5) and are particularly spectacular in autumn as the leaves turn. This area was a favourite of the composer Gustav Holst, who often used to come here to walk. He dedicated his memorable melody for the hymn 'In the Bleak Midwinter' to Cranham.

Much of the woodland this walk explores is a maze of official and unofficial paths. Please be particularly careful in following the directions.

1. Continue on the track uphill. At a complex junction after 100 yards turn left to follow a rising path for about 1/4 mile to a T-junction.

2. Turn right and after 25 yards, as the main path bends to the right, take a path on the left marked with yellow arrows. When the path forks after another 30 yards bear right and follow the path steeply uphill to the road.

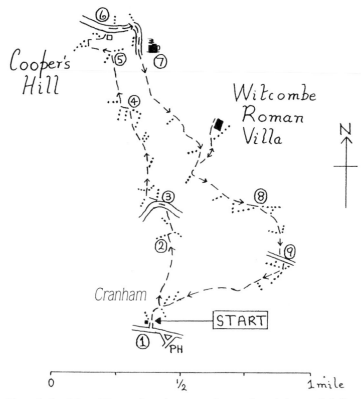

Cooper's Hill

Witcombe Roman Villa

N

Cranham

START

PH

0   ½   1 mile

3. Turn left. After 50 yards take a track on the right and follow this, ignoring a path on the right after 20 yards. Bear right just before a gate into a yard and after a further 40 yards take the centre one of three paths. Follow this, bearing left at all forks, to a T-junction with a cross-path.

4. Turn left, passing the 'Nature Reserve' notice. Ignore a path on the left after 20 yards. After a further 50 yards turn right on a wooden walkway over a boggy area. Follow the path ahead to the maypole on the edge of the slope.

This spur on the western edge of the Cotswolds gives magnificent views out over the Severn valley. The steep hill is the home of the famous cheese rolling races which take place on spring bank holiday Monday. Contestants chase 7lb Gloucester cheeses down the slope and, although the cheese inevitably reaches the bottom before it is seized, the winner is the one who arrives soon after. The prize is, of course, a cheese.

5. Turn left along the fence and follow the path downhill, turning right and right again to a small car park just underneath the maypole.

6. Turn left through the car park and then right along the lane, following the Cotswold Way signs. Bear left when the lane forks and the tea garden is on the left after 130 yards.

7. After tea continue along the lane which soon becomes a track. This is part of the Cotswold Way and is waymarked. A track on the left after $^1/_2$ mile leads down to the Great Witcombe Roman Villa. After visiting the villa, if you wish to, retrace your steps to the track and continue along it, ignoring several paths on the right.

This 1st-century villa was built into a sheltered spot on the spring line below the Cotswold escarpment. It was rediscovered in the early 1800s by workmen who were digging up an ash tree and has been periodically investigated since. Excavation has suggested that there was an earlier Iron Age settlement on the site and Cooper's Hill Farm still stands nearby, so people have lived in this favoured spot for 2,000 years at the very least.

One reason is the springs, which give an abundant supply of fresh water, although these also make the subsoil somewhat unstable and would have caused the Roman inhabitants problems. Excavations show that the villa had to be constantly buttressed and rebuilt. Despite this it was occupied until the 4th century. Some of the most important rooms with their central heating system and a mosaic pavement with dolphins and seahorses are protected under cover. They can be seen on occasional open days on summer weekends. (Further information available from the Cotswolds Countryside Service on 01452 425674.)

8. About 600 yards after the track to the villa, the wood on the left thins to a line of trees and you are level with reservoirs below. At this point bear right along a prominent track and follow it up to a road.

9. Take a path 25 yards to the left as far as a surfaced track. Turn right and after 40 yards, where short posts on the right end, bear right on a path and follow this down through the wood to the complex junction near the start and thence back to the post office.

7

BUSCOT and LECHLADE

This walk, while not the shortest in the book by any means, must be the easiest as it is completely level. Close study of the map has convinced me it climbs 9 ft over the whole distance, the biggest hill being the bridge over the river at Lechlade. The route begins at the popular beauty spot of Buscot Weir on the Thames and goes along the river bank to Kelmscott, home of the influential Victorian, William Morris. It then cuts across the fields to Lechlade for tea before returning to the start along the Thames. The walk takes you into three counties – Gloucestershire, Oxfordshire and Wiltshire!
Distance: 6 miles.

☕♥ The Café in Lechlade is unusual for a teashop because it is above a wine shop. It is most attractive with reproductions of old advertisements adorning the walls. There are some tables outside but no waitress service. They offer a good range of cakes, and cream teas are served. Light lunches of salads, filled jacket potatoes or sandwiches are available together with a range of traditional puddings. The Café is open every day throughout the year between 9 am and 5 pm, opening at 11 am on Sundays. Telephone: 01367 253990.

Teas are also served in the village shop in Buscot.

Starting point: The National Trust car park at Buscot (GR 232976).

How to get there: Take the A417 Lechlade to Faringdon road to Buscot village. From the main road turn into the village to the National Trust car park for Buscot Weir on the right.

Map: OS Landranger 163 Cheltenham and Cirencester area.

Alternative starting point: If you want to have tea at the beginning or end of the walk, start in Lechlade, parking in the town. The teashop is in the centre, on the road to Burford and Stow. You would now start the walk at point 10.

The Walk

Buscot is the estate village for Buscot Park, an 18th-century house and park nearby, and all is now in the care of the National Trust. Most of the buildings were rebuilt or much restored in the 1930s.

1. Return to the road and turn right. Bear right at the fork, to the river Thames, which here has two weirs and a lock. Cross the first weir and the lock. Immediately over the lock turn right to a stile and then head across to the far left-hand corner of a field and a bridge over the river. (Note: do not cross the bridge over the second weir.)

2. Over the river, turn right on the towpath for about 1 mile.

3. A few yards after a footbridge across the river the path comes to a stile. Immediately over the stile, turn left and walk along the left-hand side of the first field, across a bridge and along the right-hand side of a second field. At the end of the second field turn right on a hedged path and follow this round to emerge on a lane in Kelmscott by the Plough.

William Morris came to Kelmscott (pronounced Kemscot and variously spelt with one or two 't's) in 1871 and lived there until he died in 1896. The Manor House which he made his home is open to the public on Wednesdays in April to September from 11 am until 1 pm and from 2 pm until 5 pm (telephone: 01367 52486).

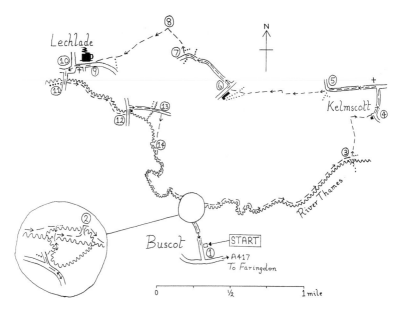

4. Turn left. At a T-junction turn left again.

The church on the right claims not to have altered since 1550 and has traces of medieval wall paintings. The grave of William Morris and his wife Jane are in the churchyard, to the right of the path, almost hidden behind some bushes.

5. After 600 yards, when the road bends sharply right, take an unsigned path on the left. This leaves the road 10 yards after a track on the left. The path is not always clear on the ground: it bears diagonally right across the field to a stile. Follow this path across two more fields. It is not always very obvious on the ground but it is quite easy to navigate between gates and stiles. In the fourth field bear slightly right to a stile onto a lane just to the left of some farm buildings.

6. Turn right. After 50 yards turn left on a narrow lane.

7. By the entrance gates to Lechlade Mill, opposite some farm buildings, turn right on a track. After 30 yards, as it bends right, leave it and continue in the same direction to a stile. Then keep on in the same direction along the left-hand side of a field as far as a stile on the left.

38

8. Over the stile, head half-right to join a concrete track and continue by the side of a wood. After a cattle grid cross a stile on the right and continue in the same direction across a field and a sports field to a road.

9. Turn right. The teashop is on the corner at the T-junction.

Lechlade stands at the confluence of three rivers, the Thames, the Leach and the Coln. It takes its name from one, the Leach, and its fame comes from the Thames as it stands just above the river's highest lock and is almost at the limit of navigation. In the past it was an important river port and much of the stone quarried near Burford was sent down river through Lechlade to build St Paul's Cathedral and many other buildings in London and Oxford. Today, it is a popular destination of pleasure boats.

The town is centred on the small, triangular market square, dominated by the parish church and overlooked by attractive mainly 18th and 19th-century buildings from the time when Lechlade was a stop on the coach routes as well as a busy port. The church is worth a look as it has some interesting monuments. As usual, there is more information available within. Shelley was inspired to write his 'Summer Evening Meditation' in 1815 in the churchyard.

10. From the teashop turn left along the main road. At the traffic lights turn left along Thames Street and cross the bridge over the river.

This bridge was built in the 18th century and is called Halfpenny Bridge from the days when there was a halfpenny toll.

11. Immediately over the bridge take a path on the right down to the river bank and turn right under the bridge. Walk along the path on the river bank to St John's Lock and the road.

St John's Lock is the highest on the Thames. There has been a bridge here since 1229 though the present structure is mainly Victorian. The Trout Inn is on the site of a medieval priory dedicated to St John the Baptist.

12. Turn left over the river. Immediately after the Trout Inn turn right on the B4449, signed 'Kelmscot 2'.

13. Some 100 yards after the bridge over the river Leach take a public footpath on the right, back to the river bank.

14. Continue along the river path to Buscot Weir. From Buscot Weir retrace your steps back to the start.

8

COLN ST ALDWYNS and ARLINGTON

This deservedly popular walk is one of the longer ones in this book. However, it is not particularly arduous and is highly recommended. The outward leg has fine views extending over the Thames valley and on a clear day the Berkshire Downs beyond can be seen. After visiting the twin villages of Arlington and Bibury on the banks of the river Coln, the walk returns along the Coln valley through delightful watermeadows and woods to the start at Coln St Aldwyns. Distance: 6 miles.

There has been a mill on the banks of the river Coln at Arlington since at least the time of the Domesday Book. The present building dates from the 17th century. Today it houses an excellent teashop and gift shop, as well as a museum tracing the history of the

mill, with guided tours of the working machinery. There is a delightful terrace outside by the river. The teashop prides itself on its home-made food and serves cream teas and a good selection of cakes. Lunches are available too and the menu is tailored to the weather. On colder days soup and hot meals, such as bangers and mash, are featured and sandwiches are always available. The trout pâté is a great favourite. The whole complex is open between 10 am and 6 pm every day and closes just on Wednesdays in January.
Telephone: 01285 740368.

When the teashop is closed there are several other sources of refreshment in Arlington and Bibury, including other teashops, most notably the Jenny Wren opposite Arlington Row, and pubs.

Starting point: Coln St Aldwyns post office and shop (GR 146052).

How to get there: From the B4425 Burford to Bibury road near Aldsworth take a minor road south, signed 'Coln St Aldwyns 2'. There are several places in the village.

Map: OS Landranger 163 Cheltenham and Cirencester.

Alternative starting point: If you want to visit the teashop at the beginning or end of the walk, start in Arlington or its twin village, Bibury, where there are several parking spots. Arlington Mill is on the main road, the B4425, just by the river. You would now start the walk at point 6.

The Walk

1. Walk down through the village and across the river.

This charming village takes its unusual name from the hermit Saint Ealdwine, to whom the church, passed at the end of the walk, was originally dedicated.

2. Immediately after the river take a public bridleway through a gate on the right. Go through a second gate and continue on the bridleway ahead, uphill. At the top bear right through a gate and follow the clear path, soon with a wall on the left, to a gate. After the gate go on in the same direction across two fields.

3. Passing some cottages on the right and barns on the left, continue to a gate. Now bear slightly left towards a house to reach a gate onto a lane.

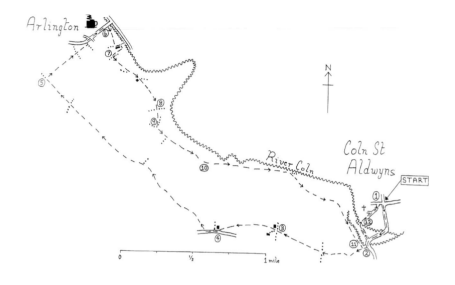

4. Turn right. After 200 yards take a public footpath along a track on the right. Follow the clear track for 1½ miles, crossing a wide path after 1¼ miles.

Just after the track starts to descend it crosses the route of Akeman Street. This important Roman road ran between St Albans and the provincial capital of Cirencester and on to Bath. Unlike many other Roman roads, such as the Foss Way, it has not really survived as part of the road network though parts are used as stretches of modern minor roads.

5. Where electricity wires cross the track two fields after this junction, turn right on an unsigned path to walk, with a hedge on the left, across two fields to another track. Cross the stile directly opposite and walk along the left-hand side of a field, passing to the right of a BT building, to a stile by a gate at the far end. Cross the stile to the road and turn right through the village of Arlington. The teashop is on the left at Arlington Mill, just before the river.

There has been a mill on this spot for at least 1,000 years; we know this because it is mentioned in the Domesday Book compiled in 1086. The present building dates from the 17th century. When the wool industry was thriving in the Cotswolds it was used for both fulling (or washing) fleeces and grinding corn. When the industry declined in the 18th century, it was given over fully to corn. In the 20th century this sort of small scale milling started to decline as well and during the First World War the mill was stripped, the steel being used for armaments. It was bought by the trout farm next door and the water that had driven the huge wheel for so long was diverted. For many years it lay neglected, being used as a store. In 1966 it was bought by David Verney, a writer and conservationist, who lovingly restored it. The original machinery had been removed, of course, but contemporary equipment was brought from North Cerney. A replacement water wheel was found. At the time of writing this is not working but there are plans to repair it and bring it into use though probably it will not be powerful enough to drive the machinery unaided. Next door to the mill, the trout farm is still going strong and 'catch your own' fishing is available.

Arlington is one of twin villages straddling the river Coln. Across the river is Bibury, a real tourist mecca since William Morris did it the service (or disservice?) of describing it, with some justification, as 'the most beautiful village in the Cotswolds'. It is well worth diverting from the route and crossing the river to explore. The creeper-covered Swan Hotel has long been a favourite with fishermen and before that with the visitors who flocked here in King Charles II's time for Bibury Races. The small building with no windows close by was the local lock-up. The village is centred on a square with fine old cottages and an ancient church, which is basically Saxon with, of course, many later additions and alterations. Some of the grave slabs were such fine examples that they were taken to the British Museum and what we view now are casts. See inside the church for more information.

6. After tea, take a path across the road from the teashop. Just past some cottages take a path on the right which goes through a small parking area before going up some steps.

The chocolate box row of 17th-century weavers' cottages, much admired and photographed, is called Arlington Row and is now in the care of the National Trust. The watermeadow they face, now a protected breeding ground for wildfowl, is known as Rack Isle. The wool, fulled at the mill and woven in the cottages, was stretched out here on racks to dry.

7. At the top of the steps turn left to follow the main path through the woods. At a fork, bear left to a stone stile. Over the stile continue by the wall and then, at a cricket pavilion, bear half-right down to a stile at the far end of the field. The path is not apparent on the ground at this point.

8. Follow the path through the wood to a stile. Over the stile, the path is again not apparent on the ground but continues ahead, with a wall on the right, to another stile and then to a track.

9. Turn right and then shortly turn left at a T-junction of tracks. When the track bends right, take a track on the left to continue in the same direction. When the track ends continue along the left-hand side of a field and then a fenced path to a gate and stile.

10. Now bear half-left to a metal gate. Follow the path by the river and stay on the signed path as it veers right, away from the river.

11. At the road turn left. After crossing the river, turn left again, continuing on a track when the surfaced lane turns into an entrance.

12. Just before some gates across the track, cross the river by a footbridge and follow the path, which soon becomes a lane, back to Coln St Aldwyns.

The church, passed on the left, was originally dedicated to St Ealdwine. In the 13th century it changed to the unusual and rather gruesome Decollation of St John the Baptist – the word decollation means beheading. There are some fine gargoyles on the outside of the tower including one of the devil chasing a man with the man's hand in his jaws. John Keble, father of the John Keble of Oxford fame, was vicar here from 1782 until 1835 and his son was curate for the last ten of those years.

9

NORTHLEACH

This is a very easy, almost level stroll to the old wool town of Northleach, the undoubted highlight of the walk. Northleach is an interesting place to visit with many fascinating things to see, including a unique musical museum, a magnificent church, often referred to as the 'Cathedral of the Cotswolds', and a glimpse of life in the past. It is a charming town with a high proportion of attractive old buildings in Cotswold stone. Be sure to allow plenty of time! Distance: 4 miles.

The Corner Green Restaurant and Tea Shop is to be found in a building dating from the 1700s, almost in the centre of Northleach. It serves an excellent range of delicious cakes as well as cream teas. For a substantial lunch there are grills and two home-made hot dishes every day, and for a lighter meal you will find sandwiches, soup and jacket potatoes. The teashop is open from 10 am to 5 pm on weekdays and 9 am to 5.30 pm at weekends. It is closed on Mondays. Telephone: 01451 860240.

Starting point: Hampnett church (GR 100157).

How to get there: From the A40 Oxford to Cheltenham road, 1 mile west of the junction with the A429 take a minor road, signed 'Hampnett only'. Park near the church.

Map: OS Landranger 163 Cheltenham and Cirencester area.

Alternative starting point: If you want to visit the teashop at the beginning or end of the walk, start in Northleach, parking in the town centre. The teashop is opposite the World of Mechanical Music. You would now commence at point 9.

The Walk

The delightful village of Hampnett is centred on a field-like village green which gives rise to one of the Cotswolds' loveliest streams, the Leach. The little church is largely Norman and it is well worth a look to make up your own mind about the startling Victorian restoration work carried out by the then incumbent, the Reverend W. Wiggins, in the 1870s. Some think that it is an imaginative and daring recreation of what a church like this would have been like in the past; others are appalled by it and consider that it detracts from the clean Norman lines of the building. More information is available within.

Hampnett achieved a certain fame, not to say notoriety, in the 17th century when a family called Hughes made it the Gretna Green of the London–Gloucester road and an unusually high number of marriages were recorded about then.

1. With your back to the church turn left. At Manor Farm turn left again and when the track forks after 10 yards bear left to walk on a concrete track, with a stone wall on the left and barns on the right.

2. Go through a metal field gate ahead and bear half-left across the field to a stile.

3. Turn left along the A40 then turn right on a minor road. After 90

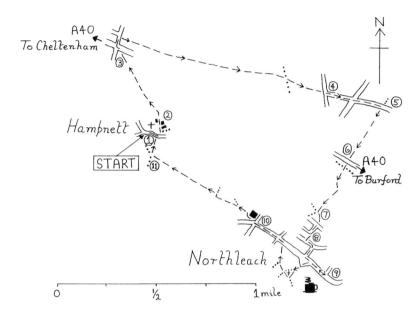

yards, opposite a road junction, turn right on a track. Follow this for about a mile to a lane. It starts as a track, becomes more of a path and then becomes more definitely a track again.

4. Take the lane opposite and continue across the A429.

The A429 follows the route of the Foss Way, the Roman road that runs diagonally across the Cotswolds through Moreton-in-Marsh, Stow-on-the-Wold and Cirencester on its way between Lincoln and Exeter.

5. Some 250 yards after the junction take a public footpath on the right, signed 'Northleach'. The footpath goes straight along the right-hand side of the field to the A40.

6. Cross the A40 and take the footpath directly opposite. Go straight ahead to a stile and cross a track to continue on the footpath along the right-hand side of a field. The clear path soon bends right to Northleach, seen ahead.

7. After the second stile bear left to another stile. At the road go ahead along Mays Crescent opposite and when the road soon bends right, continue in the same direction on a path between houses.

8. At the lane turn left. Turn right at a metal gate and follow the road to Market Place. Turn left for the teashop, which is a couple of hundred yards ahead on the right, opposite the World of Mechanical Music.

Northleach was established in 1230 by the Abbot of Gloucester as a trading place strategically sited midway between Cirencester and Stow-on-the-Wold. It succeeded so well that by the 15th century it was an important international market for wool. The merchants who made their fortunes through this trade displayed their wealth and saved their souls by contributing to the church and throughout the Cotswolds there are many outstanding 'wool' churches. The church of St Peter and St Paul in Northleach is one of the finest, having in particular outstanding brasses. More information is available inside.

There are many attractive buildings from the 16th to 19th centuries here. One of them houses the World of Mechanical Music, where automata, clocks and music boxes from all over the world are displayed, and also repaired. The ticket includes a one-hour guided tour. It is open every day except Christmas Day (telephone: 01451 60181).

9. From the teashop return to Market Place and take the path to the church from the top of the square. Leave the churchyard (not the new graveyard) at the top right-hand corner through the metal kissing-gate and follow the path across to and between houses to the road. Turn left to the crossroads with the A429.

At the crossroads is the old police station and prison built by Sir George Onesiphorus Paul in 1790. He was a member of a family of Huguenot clothiers from Woodchester and had very advanced views about prisons in his day, seeing them not just as lock-ups but as houses of correction. In the cells is a display about prisons in the 18th century and Paul's ideas. The building also houses an interesting museum illustrating aspects of rural life. It is open between April and October from 10 am (2 pm on Sunday) until 5 pm and there is also a tourist information centre, shop and tearoom (telephone: 01451 860715).

10. Take the road opposite. After 40 yards cross a stile on the right. Follow the clear path along the right-hand side of the first field and then the left-hand side of the second field. Through the gate at the far end, continue in the same direction across two more fields.

11. Turn right along the track, back to the start.

10

SWINBROOK and BURFORD

This walk is a delightful and easy stroll between a picture postcard village which has produced famous (not to say notorious) daughters and an ancient town full of interest. The return leg, after tea in Burford, is along the bank of the river Windrush and is particularly charming. The walk could easily be turned into a church crawl as it passes three old churches, all very different and all interesting.
Distance: 4¹/₂ miles.

Huffkins, 98 The High Street, Burford is a classic teashop and bakery with a garden behind. The building is over 400 years old and it has been a bakery for the last 50 years. All the delicious cakes and pastries are made on the premises under the supervision of the master baker. The cream teas include lashings of clotted cream or you can choose something from the shop to enjoy with your tea. One particular favourite is a bee sting! This is a brioche with cream, custard and honey. Light lunches are served. Something delicious and unusual is toast williams which is ham, pears and grated cheese melted under the grill. It is open every day all year between 9 am and and 5 pm. Telephone: 01993 822126.

When Huffkins is closed, there are several other sources of refreshment in Burford including the Priory Tea Shop further down High Street on the right-hand side towards the river.

Starting point: Swinbrook (GR 281121).

How to get there: From the A40 some 6 miles west of Witney take a minor road northwards, signed 'Swinbrook 1' and continue to the village. There are some spots where it is possible to park, near the telephone box.

Map: OS Landranger 163 Cheltenham and Cirencester.

Alternative starting point: If you want to visit the teashop at the beginning or end of the walk, start in Burford where there is a public car park near the church, signed from High Street. You would now commence at point 7.

The Walk

Swinbrook was the home of one of the great Oxfordshire families, the Fettiplaces. Nothing remains of their great manor house between the church and the river Windrush but they are remembered by their amazing memorial in St Mary's, which it is well worth taking time to see. The north wall of the chancel of this mainly 13th- to 15th-century church is taken up with two tiers of effigies of male Fettiplaces. Three Tudor knights lie stiffly on their sides, each with their head resting on one hand, looking out across the centuries at us. Next to them are three more from the 17th century, more relaxed and each propped on one elbow.

In the churchyard is a row of handsome table tombs in the best Cotswold tradition. Near the porch are the Cotswold stone headstones commemorating two members of an eccentric Swinbrook family rather better remembered today. Two of the six Mitford sisters, Nancy and Unity, are buried here in

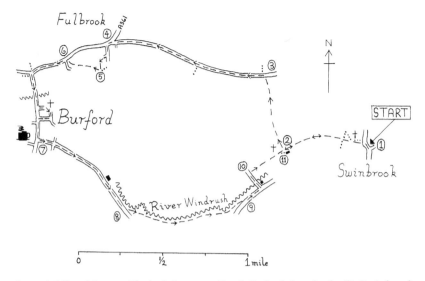

their childhood home. Their father was Lord Redesdale who built Swinbrook House a mile north of the village in the 1920s. Their life was described by Nancy in her first novel, 'The Pursuit of Love', and by their sister Jessica in her book 'Hons and Rebels'. It seems that things were rarely dull – for example, printed notices in the guest rooms apparently read, 'Owing to an unidentified corpse in the cistern visitors are requested not to drink the bath water'. Unity was devoted to Hitler and tried unsuccessfully to commit suicide by shooting herself in the head when the Second World War was declared.

1. Take the path signed 'Widford ³/₄' next to the Old Post Office. It goes initially between houses, then walls, and then in the same direction across fields to the little church seen ahead.

2. Before reaching the church, immediately after an isolated house on the left, turn right on a signed footpath to a stile by a gate. Follow the path across the field to another stile by a gate onto a lane.

3. Turn left. As you walk along this quiet lane, Burford comes into view on the left.

4. At the A361 turn left. At the war memorial, after 50 yards turn left again. After 70 yards, opposite the entrance to Elm Farm House, now a hotel, turn right and follow the track, keeping to the right of Mullions, to a stile.

This village is Fulbrook and was home to an infamous Tom, Dick and Harry, in this case the Dunsdon brothers. Sons of a respectable family, they became highwaymen preying on the Oxford–Gloucester coach. They plotted to rob the nearby manor of Tangley Hall and the constables learned of their plan. There was a hole in the door of Tangley Manor for inspecting visitors, normally guarded by a shutter. This was removed on the night of the robbery and when an arm appeared it was lassoed and tied to the door handle. Suddenly, after much swearing and shouting from outside, the arm dropped through the hole onto the floor. The brothers had escaped but Dick was never seen again and it was assumed he had died after the severing of his arm. The remaining two continued in their life of crime but were eventually arrested and hanged in Gloucester. After their execution the bodies were brought back and displayed on a local gibbet.

5. Over the stile, turn immediately left to another one. Over this, turn right to a stile onto a fenced path leading to a metal kissing-gate. Walk along the left-hand side of a small field to a stile by a small gate and then to the left of a garage to rejoin the A361.

6. Turn left. At the road junction turn left into Burford, crossing the river. Go left along Lawrence Lane to the churchyard, which you then leave by the gate opposite the main door. Turn right opposite the almshouses and left at the High Street. The teashop is on the right up the High Street.

Burford is an old town, full of interest and history wherever you look. In Saxon times it was an important river crossing and a market grew up the slope from the river. By the early Middle Ages it was an established town with narrow plots running back from the broad street where the market was held. Today these have been replaced by an attractive jumble of houses and shops, many of them now selling antiques. Burford has always been quick to seize a commercial opportunity. For 200 years races held over the seven downs to the south-west brought gentlefolk and gamblers, riff-raff and royalty to the town. Among the latter was Charles II and his pretty, witty Nell Gwynne. Their son, born in 1670, was made Earl of Burford and Nell called her rooms at Windsor 'Burford House'.

The church is crammed with fascinating historic objects and memorials; there is an excellent booklet to guide you round and also an interesting leaflet about the Levellers. These were disaffected soldiers in Cromwell's New Model Army who mutinied in 1649. After their capture they were held in Burford church and eventually three of their number were shot against the church wall as an example to the rest. One of them, Anthony Sedley, passed the time carving his name on the font and it can still be seen.

7. From the teashop take Witney Street, almost opposite, and follow it out of the town.

8. Some 250 yards after Springfield House take a public footpath on the left, signed 'Widford 1', bearing right towards and then along the river bank. The path basically follows the river to a metal gate onto a road, sometimes cutting across bends.

9. Turn left along the lane. Turn left again at Widford Mill Farm and continue.

10. Turn right over a cattle grid on a public footpath, signed 'Swinbrook 1', and follow the track to St Oswald's church, passed earlier and now seen ahead.

St Oswald's church is a complete contrast to the two visited earlier in the walk. It is all that remains of a deserted medieval village except for humps in the field next to it. St Oswald was a King of Northumbria who was killed in battle by Penda of Mercia in AD 642. His body rested here on its way back to Lindisfarne for burial and the church was built on the floor of a Roman villa. This used to be visible but has now been covered up to conserve it until a full excavation can take place. The church was not used after the middle of the 19th century and fell into serious disrepair. It was restored in 1904, when the Roman pavement and medieval wall paintings were discovered.

11. Pass the church on the left to retrace the path to the start.

11

WINCHCOMBE and HAILES ABBEY

This walk is full of fascinating things to see, both ancient and modern, and so it could easily make a full day's expedition. It starts at the headquarters of the Gloucestershire and Warwickshire Railway at Toddington and wends its way along the base of the Cotswold Edge to the ancient town of Winchcombe, once capital of the kingdom of Mercia. On the way, it passes the ruins of Hailes Abbey and a stop to explore these is highly recommended. Nearby is a fascinating old church of even greater antiquity. After tea at Winchcombe the return is made on the restored railway to the starting point. Trains run every weekend from March to November and there are Santa Specials in December. In addition, there are trains most days in July and August. The railway operates a talking timetable on 01242 621405.
Distance: 5 miles plus train ride back to start.

The building which houses the Olde Bakery Tea Shoppe is 200 to 300 years old and was a bakery earlier this century. It is now a superb tea stop, with two tearooms, a glass conservatory and a charming patio garden. A number of set teas are offered, including the Old Bakery Tea with boiled eggs and the Summertime Tea with cucumber sandwiches. There are special suggestions for children, such as the Yummy Tum Tea with baked beans, as well as an excellent selection of cakes and other temptations, all home-made. At lunchtime there is always a selection of hot dishes, with a vegetarian option, as well as lighter meals like filled jacket potatoes and sandwiches. It is open throughout the year until 5 pm on Tuesday to Sunday and bank holiday Mondays.
Telephone: 01242 602469.

Refreshments are also served at the railway café, the Flag and Whistle, at Toddington.

Starting point: The GWR station at Toddington (GR 050323).

How to get there: From the A435 Evesham to Cheltenham road take the B4077 towards Stow. Follow the brown signs for the GWR Steam Centre, where there is a large car park.

Map: OS Landranger 150 Worcester and the Malverns.

Alternative starting point: If you want to visit the teashop at the beginning or end of the walk, start in Winchcombe. The Olde Bakery is on the High Street, the main road through the town. The best car park to use is the one on Back Lane, near the library which is the long-stay car park. You would now commence at point 10.

The Walk

1. Return to the road and turn right. Just after the bridge over the railway and some cottages take a path on the right. Follow this path by the railway from stile to stile. To the left are excellent views of the Cotswold Edge.

2. At a lane turn left and continue to a T-junction, ignoring paths on the right.

3. Turn right for 100 yards. As the road bends right, take a path on the left to continue in the same direction across a field. The path is not

55

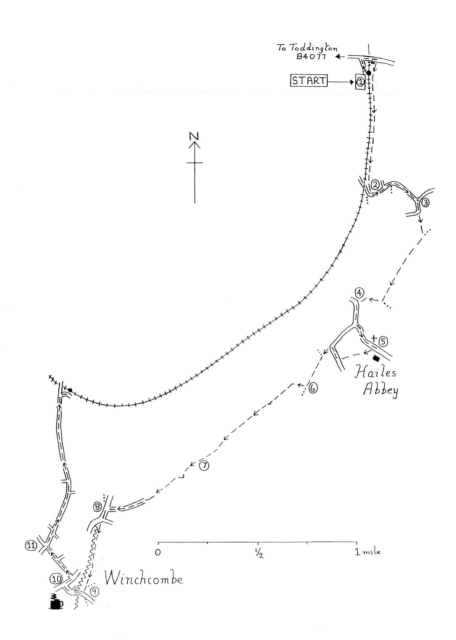

To Toddington
B4077

START

N

Hailes
Abbey

Winchcombe

0   ½   1 mile

apparent on the ground but bears away from the hedge on the left to lead to a stile by a large oak tree. Over the stile, turn right and walk along the right-hand side of the field, then follow the clear path round to the right towards some farm buildings.

4. At a lane turn left. At a T-junction turn left to Hailes Abbey.

In 1242 Richard, Earl of Cornwall, was returning to England from a crusade. His ship was nearly wrecked and he vowed that if he survived he would show his gratitude by founding an abbey. Building started in 1245 and monks came to found a Cistercian monastery. The abbey was dedicated in 1251 in a glittering ceremony attended by the king and queen. Richard's son Edmund guaranteed the wealth and prosperity of the abbey by the gift of a phial of Holy Blood authenticated by Pope Urban IV. Pilgrims flocked but only those not in a state of sin could see it. Fortunately for the prosperity of the abbey, sin could be washed away by absolution and gifts to the church. When the relic was examined just before dissolution it was found to be coloured gum. It was said that the glass phial was thicker on one side than the other. The thick side was opaque so the monks could control who saw the blood – it was only revealed to those who had sufficiently expiated their sin.

The abbey was dissolved in 1539, stripped of its treasure and sold. Parts were used as a private house and it was plundered for building stone, leaving the romantic ruin we see today. It came into the care of the government in 1948. Today's visitor can hire a self-guided taped tour and this is very strongly recommended, but be warned that it takes about an hour. The abbey is open between 10 am and 4 pm all year, extending to 6 pm in summer. Admission is free to members of the National Trust and English Heritage.

Opposite the abbey is the parish church, which predates it and has some remarkable medieval wall paintings. The colours have faded and bits are missing but enough remains to show how vibrant the works must have been when they were new.

5. After exploring the abbey return to the lane and turn left for a few yards. Take a path on the left, signed 'Cotswold Way, Winchcombe 3km'. Bear right across the field to a gate in the far corner and along a track. At a lane turn right and then left along a track, following the Cotswold Way signs.

6. After about ¼ mile turn right on a path signed 'Cotswold Way'. Start along the right-hand side of the field and about halfway along turn left across it. Cut across the corner of the next field to a metal

kissing-gate and then continue in the same direction to another one. Keep going in the same direction and at the brow of the rise Winchcombe comes into view ahead. The path is clear and waymarked with the Cotswold Way sign of a yellow arrow and white dot.

7. The path soon joins a track which steadily improves and is eventually surfaced.

8. At a road turn left. Just after Rushley Lane take a path on the left, initially by the river Isbourne and then across two footbridges and by some houses to a road.

9. Turn right. The teashop is at a road junction ahead on the left corner.

Winchcombe has a different, and longer, history from most Cotswold towns; by the time most of them were reaching their height of wealth and importance through the wool trade, Winchcombe's greatest days were over.

It was one of the seats of the royalty of the Saxon kingdom of Mercia. The story goes that when King Kenulf, founder of the abbey, died in AD 819 he was succeeded by his son Kenelm, who was said to be only seven at the time. His scheming and ambitious sister Quendryth persuaded her lover, the boy's tutor, to kill him and this he did on a hunting trip by cutting off his head with a long knife. Monks went from the abbey to bring the body home, guided to his grave by a shaft of light. Wherever it rested on the way home, a spring gushed out. As it was being taken to its final resting place beside Kenulf, his sister looked out of a window and her eyes fell out of their sockets, proving her guilt.

The story became the stuff of legend and Kenelm was made a saint and martyr, which greatly added to the eventual prosperity of the abbey. When the abbey foundations were excavated in 1815 two stone coffins were found side by side, one containing the skeleton of a man and the other the bones of a child. With the latter was a large knife, so there might be some grain of truth behind the legend. The coffins are now in the church. Quendryth went on to become Abbess of Southminster but it is not known whether she was blind.

The abbey was a Benedictine house and became rich and powerful, a centre of academic excellence. The citizens of Winchcombe had a love–hate relationship with it, loving the income that the accommodation and entertaining of pilgrims and visiting scholars brought but seeing it as a grasping landlord. For example, in 1231 the bells of the town church were rung deliberately to disturb the monks' services. The end came for the abbey in 1539. The lead was stripped from the roof and most of the buildings were destroyed. By the 18th century nothing could be seen above ground and the site now lies on private ground. Winchcombe was plunged into poverty by the removal of its main source of income and did not really recover for hundreds of years. This can be seen in the modesty of much of its architecture compared with the affluent Cotswold wool towns. Charters for fairs were granted but this did not really rescue the town. A small revival came with tobacco growing but this was made illegal in 1640 to protect the industry in the new found colony of Virginia. This prohibition led to rioting, to no avail.

The church was built around 1470 when Winchcombe was at its height. On the outside walls is a wonderfully ugly array of gargoyles sometimes called the Winchcombe Worthies. In view of sometimes tense relations between the town and the abbey, it is possible they are caricatures of unpopular monks.

10. From the teashop turn right along the main road, then left along North Street.

11. Turn right along Greet Road by the police station. Just before the bridge over the railway, turn right to the station and take the train back to the start.

This line was built in the 1900s, connecting Birmingham with Cheltenham via Stratford-on-Avon. Traffic dwindled in the 1960s, then the line was closed in 1977 and the track lifted. The Gloucestershire and Warwickshire Railway bought 15 miles of trackbed in 1984 and have rebuilt a short section connecting Toddington and Winchcombe and on through the Greet tunnel. This stretches for 693 yards and is one of the longest on any preserved railway in Britain. If you have time, you can ride down through the tunnel and for a mile further to the present limit of the line before going back to Toddington, where the station has been restored and there is a shop and café.

12

BOURTON-ON-THE-WATER

No book of walks to teashops in the Cotswolds would be complete without a visit to Bourton-on-the-Water where it seems that every second building in the centre of the town serves teas. This is not surprising as it is probably the most visited tourist honeypot in the Cotswolds. Do not let that detract you from this attractive and mainly level walk which is mostly on very quiet paths and lanes.
Distance: 4 miles.

Until the 1960s the building housing Small Talk Tea Shop was a blacksmith's. It is now a delightful traditional tea rooms with an excellent selection of delicious cakes. Other tea-time goodies include scones with clotted cream, crumpets with honey, and toasted teacakes.

For a light lunch there is a choice of sandwiches and filled jacket potatoes. They are open from 10 am until 4.30 pm every day throughout the year.
Telephone: 01451 821596.

When the teashop is closed there are numerous other tea places, restaurants and pubs in Bourton-on-the-Water.

Starting point: Lower Slaughter church (GR 166225).

How to get there: From the A429 Stow-on-the-Wold to Cirencester road 3 miles south of Stow take the minor road westwards, signed 'The Slaughters'. Park near the church.

Map: OS Landranger 163 Cheltenham and Cirencester area.

Alternative starting point: If you want to visit the teashop at the beginning or end of the walk, start in Bourton-on-the-Water, where there is ample parking in the town car park. You would now commence at the end of point 6, taking the path to the village from the car park.

The Walk

1. From the church gate and facing the river, turn left to walk along the road, with the water on the right. When the river soon bends away, continue along the road.

Despite its rather grim name, Lower Slaughter is a picture postcard village. The explanation of the name varies according to which authority you consult. Some say that it comes from the Saxon for the place of the sloe trees, others that it means the place of the pools. Yet a third explanation is that it derives from slough or muddy place where cattle crossed the river Eye, now confined between neat walls and trimmed lawns. The church was rebuilt in 1867 and its most interesting feature is the fibreglass top given to the spire in 1968.

2. By the entrance to The Whitmores, as the road bends right, continue in the same direction on a track. After 50 yards, at the end of a wooden fence on the right, go through a small wooden gate on the right and across the garden of Four Wells, between sheds to a stile into a field. Go diagonally across the field to a gate in the far left-hand corner and then

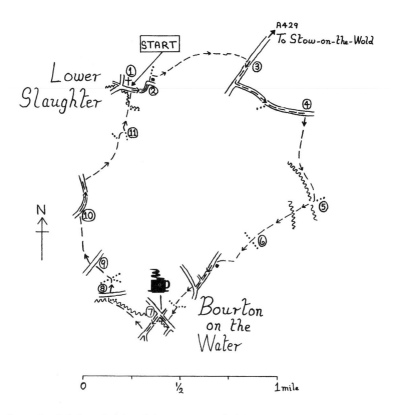

along the left-hand side of the next two fields to stiles and a bridge over a stream. Keep on the left-hand side of the next field, then over a stile and continue in the same direction, now on the right-hand side of a field to a gate onto a road. Much of this path is often not apparent on the ground.

3. Turn right. After 200 yards turn left on a lane signed 'Wyck Rissington'.

4. After about ¹/₂ mile take a path over a stile on the right. Go through the gate ahead and walk along the left-hand side of a field and then through a short fenced section to a stile. Continue along the right-hand side of the next two fields, soon walking by a stream.

5. Cross the stream when you come to the bridge on the right. The

route now joins the Oxfordshire Way for a short distance and is much more clear on the ground and well marked by blue arrows.

6. Go straight ahead across a wide cross-path, so leaving the Oxfordshire Way, which turns right here. Walk to the far end of the field to pick up a clear path going right towards the houses of Bourton-on-the-Water, seen ahead. When the path reaches the first house go down the steps to a lane and turn left. At the T-junction turn left again to a main road. Cross the road and take a path almost directly opposite. Go across the car park and along a signed path to the village to emerge on the High Street. There are teashops all around. The Small Talk Tea Shop is on the right along the High Street.

Crowds of visitors flock to Bourton, drawn by both the appeal of the town itself and its many tourist attractions. It is sometimes called the 'Blackpool of the Cotswolds', a derisive allusion to the cheerful holiday atmosphere found on sunny summer Sundays. The alternative soubriquet 'Venice of the Cotswolds' surely goes too far the other way, despite the river by the main street crossed and recrossed by graceful 18th-century bridges.

The Model Village is the oldest purpose-built tourist attraction. Opened in 1937 in the garden of the Old New Inn, it is a replica of the village to one-ninth scale, built in Cotswold stone and faithful in every detail to the original, with, of course, a model of the model behind the model of the New Old Inn!

7. After tea cross the High Street and go along Sherbourne Street beside the war memorial, passing the Duke of Wellington. At the junction with Bow Lane take a public footpath on the right and follow it beside the river to a road.

8. Turn right. After 15 yards take a public footpath on the left next to Dalmeeny Cottage. Follow the path over the disused railway and ahead to the main road.

9. Cross the road and take a public footpath directly opposite. Follow the path across two fields, bearing half-right in the second field to a lane.

10. Turn right. After 300 yards take a public bridleway through a small wooden gate on the right and walk down the left-hand side of the field.

11. At the bottom of the field turn left through a gate and follow the clear path back to Lower Slaughter.

13

STOW-ON-THE-WOLD

This easy and interesting walk can be enjoyed at any time of year but is ideal for a bright winter day. The route is largely on surfaced drives, tracks and quiet lanes, making it a good choice at times when conditions underfoot are uncomfortably muddy elsewhere. The centrepiece is the ancient market town of Stow-on-the-Wold which has several excellent teashops and numerous antique and craft shops and many a happy hour can be spent pottering about its quaint streets and alleys.
Distance: 4 miles.

The Cotswold Coffee Shop on Digbeth Street is a cheerful establishment with unusual, brightly-coloured curtains with a tea pot motif echoed in a painted border. Try to time your walk to include a lunchtime visit to enjoy the excellent range of lunch suggestions including cauliflower bake, beef stew with crusty bread

or home made soup complemented by tasty baguettes and sandwiches. This can be rounded off by tempting puddings such as rich fruit rum bread and butter pudding or traditional trifle. The tea time menu includes cream teas with clotted cream or a good choice of cakes washed down with a range of speciality teas. They are open from 10 am until 5 pm throughout the year.
Telephone: 01451 830151.

Starting point: Lower Swell (GR 176255).

How to get there: From the A429 at Stow take a minor road opposite the Unicorn Hotel, signed 'Lower Swell'. Park in some laybys on the left soon after entering the village.

Map: OS Landranger 163 Cheltenham and Cirencester area.

Alternative starting point: If you want to visit the teashop at the beginning or end of the walk, start in Stow-on-the-Wold, where there is ample parking in the town car park. You would now commence at the end of point 7, turning left into the town from the car park.

The Walk

1. Continue along the road towards the Golden Ball. Just before the pub turn left on a signed public footpath and follow the track round to a lane. Turn left.

2. Just before the end of speed limit sign bear left along a track signed 'public bridleway'. This soon comes to a complex junction of paths. Carry on in the same direction to a gate and then along the right-hand side of a field to a gate on the right.

3. Go through the gate and across a stream and then head across two fields towards some farm buildings seen ahead, noting the novel horse exercising machine on the left.

4. Turn left and follow a surfaced drive all the way to the main road.

5. Turn left, crossing to a footpath on the opposite side.

This road, now the A429, is on the route of the Roman road, the Foss Way (see walk 9). Just nearby, on private land to the right, is St Edward's Well. It is not clear with which St Edward the well is supposed to be connected – the 9th-century young king stabbed to death at Corfe Castle, the Confessor or a hermit

65

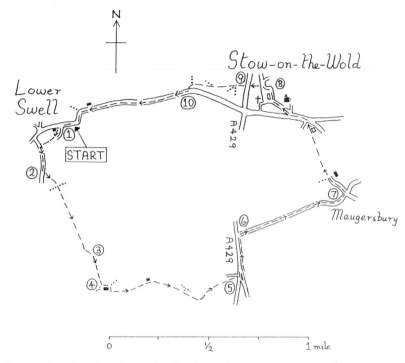

from early Christian times who lived near here.

6. After 300 yards take the first turning on the right. This lane has been blocked off at this end and so there is virtually no traffic on it.

The lane leads into the village of Maugersbury. This was a successful trading centre by the 11th century but it lost out to nearby Stow-on-the-Wold when the latter was granted a royal market charter by Henry I in 1107. Stow developed into a prosperous town while Maugersbury remained a village.

7. At a crossroads turn left between stone pillars. When the tarmac ends at Maugersbury Manor continue ahead on a track and follow this into Stow-on-the-Wold, passing a car park. When it meets a road continue in the same direction, bearing right along Digbeth Street when the road forks. Simpson's Tea Shop is on the right.

The town is centred on the large, attractive square where sheep were once bought and sold. At one end is a small grassed area with the 19th-century stocks and all around are buildings from the 17th and 18th centuries. The Talbot Hotel was built before 1714 and for a time served as the Corn Exchange. If you look on the wall you will find a brass letterbox where farmers used to post samples of corn to be tested for quality. You must make your own mind up about the Victorian Gothic-style assembly rooms in the middle, now housing the library, dividing up the square. The narrow alleys, or tures, allowed sheep to be herded into the square and counted as they went.

St Edward's church, just behind the square, was ruined in the Civil War. One of the last and fiercest battles was fought at nearby Donnington and the Royalist army was totally defeated. Over 1,000 prisoners were incarcerated in the church, which suffered much damage. Many were executed but there is only one marked grave of a soldier from the battle or its aftermath - that of Captain Keyte. The church was restored after the Civil War and again in the last century.

8. After tea continue along the road into the square and turn right. Leave by High Street at the far end. A few yards along High Street turn left along an alley next to the ladies' public lavatory.

9. Cross the road at the end and continue on a track opposite. When the track turns left go through a metal kissing-gate in the wall ahead and take a faint path ahead across a field. This soon fades out but carry on across the field to the far left corner to find another metal kissing-gate which gives onto a road.

The large house seen in the valley down to the right is Abbotswood, designed by Edward Lutyens in 1902. He was also responsible for the gardens, noted for their flower displays and shrubs, and open to the public on occasional days in the summer.

10. Turn right, back to the start.

The road passes Spa Cottages on the right. A chalybeate spring was discovered here in 1807 and there was a plan to develop a spa here to exploit it. If the plan had been successful we might now talk of Swell in the same league as Harrogate or Leamington. However, history turned out differently and we have some cottages in a tiny village instead!

14

BROADWAY

This walk climbs gently to the ancient settlement of Saintbury, partway up the Cotswold Edge. The highlight is a level path with wide views out across the plain to the Malvern Hills and beyond. The route drops down to Broadway for tea, often claimed to be the prettiest of the small Cotswold towns. The return leg is an easy stroll using quiet and level field paths at the base of the Edge. Distance: 5 miles.

Roberto's is a busy, bustling restaurant at the bottom of the High Street, looking out over the green. It serves meals, among them grills and salads and light lunches, as well as a good selection of teatime favourites, including cream teas. There is a courtyard outside which is very pleasant on warm days. It is open between 9.30 am and 7 pm every day in the summer and closed between December and March.

Telephone: 01386 858226.

There are numerous other teashops in Broadway as well as all kinds of restaurants and pubs, so you should never go hungry or thirsty here!

Starting point: Willersey village car park (GR 105395).

How to get there: The walk starts in Willersey, which is on the B4632 Stratford-upon-Avon to Broadway road. There is a car park behind the village hall, opposite the garage.

Map: OS Landranger 150 Worcester and the Malverns.

Alternative starting point: If you want to visit the teashop at the beginning or end of the walk, start in Broadway where there is ample parking in the town car park. You would now commence at point 8.

The Walk

1. Return to the main road and turn left. Opposite the pond turn right along Church Street to the church. Go into the churchyard and bear left to a wooden kissing-gate opposite the far end of the church.

There has been a church on this site since the 8th century, with rectors listed from 1281. Willersey was the summer residence of the abbots of Evesham and in the 14th and 15th centuries they enlarged the church and were responsible for its unusual cruciform shape. As usual, there is more information available within.

2. Through the gate, turn right to a stile. Bear left across a corner of a field to another stile and cross a small field to a gate. Continue along the right-hand side of the field for 45 yards then cross a stile in the fence on the right.

3. Bear diagonally left across the field and then along the left-hand side of the next two fields. Halfway up the second field cross a stile on the left and go ahead along the left-hand side of another field. When the fence on the left ends, continue straight ahead to a stile then bear slightly right to a stile in the far right-hand corner of the field.

4. Over the stile, turn left along a lane. At a T-junction turn right into Saintbury. As the road bends left take the public footpath on the right by Walnut Tree Cottage to the church.

Saintbury is a very ancient settlement. Its name comes from two Saxon words,

69

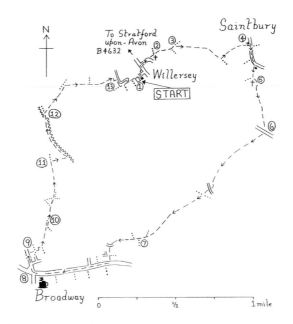

swain meaning villein and bury meaning hill. The position of the village has moved; originally it was above the church. There are excellent views from the north porch of the church, which was originally Saxon.

5. Go to the left of the church to a small gate and cross to a stile. Follow the path steeply up through a wood to a stile and then continue in the same direction along the left-hand side of a field. Note the humps and bumps showing the original site of Saintbury. When the fence ends continue in more or less the same direction, to the left of a line of trees. The path is not visible on the ground but its route is shown by a line of posts.

6. Cross a lane and take a bridleway directly opposite. This delightful level path has extensive views on the right and first a wood and then a golf course on the left. At the end of the golf course go through a gate and bear right downhill towards Broadway, seen below, soon crossing a surfaced track. Continue downhill on this attractive path to emerge near a junction of tracks.

7. Turn left. After 5 yards, at the junction, turn right. After 40 yards, as the track bends right, bear left off the track to follow a

70

path between a fence and a hedge. Cross a road and continue on the path to the main road. Turn right into Broadway. The teashop is at the far end of the High Street.

Broadway's prosperity has always depended on meeting the needs of visitors. In the 17th and 18th centuries it was an important stop on the coach route from London to Worcester. Horses had to be changed before they could tackle the steep hill to the south of the town. The most famous of the many coaching inns is the Lygon Arms. General Lygon's butler saw the great promise in what was then the White Hart Inn. He bought it from the general and renamed it after him.

8. From the teashop cross the green and take the road directly opposite, to the left of the Swan Inn. At the junction keep ahead along Springfield Lane. After 130 yards turn right along an alley next to Primrose Cottage.

9. Cross a track and take the public footpath, signed 'Willersey'. The fenced path goes around some buildings to a track. Turn left. After 200 yards go over a stile on the right by some new houses to continue in the same direction.

10. When the houses end, go over a bridge across a ditch and straight ahead across a field to a stile and small gate. Go over the stile and walk along the right-hand side of the field. As you approach the end of the field, go over a stile on the right to cross the hedge and continue in the same direction.

11. The map shows the path going straight across the next field but on the ground it lies round the right perimeter, coming to a bridge over a ditch. It then goes along the right-hand side of a field as far as a bridge over a stream. Cross the bridge and continue in the same direction to the corner of the field.

12. Turn right to walk along the left-hand side of two fields, through a scrubby strip of wood and along the left-hand side of a third field. At the end of the field turn right to a stile.

13. Cross the stile and follow the path between houses to a road. Turn right. When the road shortly bends left at a pillar box, continue on the path. At a T-junction turn left and follow the path between houses to the car park.

15

BROAD CAMPDEN and CHIPPING CAMPDEN

John Masefield sang the praises of Chipping Campden when he wrote:

'On Campden wold the skylark sings,

In Campden town the traveller finds

The inward peace that beauty brings

To bless and heal tormented minds.'

This short and easy walk, mainly on quiet field paths, from the lovely village of Broad Campden to Chipping Campden will, it is hoped, bring peace of mind and certainly a good tea.
Distance: 2½ miles.

Bantam Tea Rooms is a classic teashop in a building dating from 1693. It has a welcome open fire in winter and some tables in an attractive courtyard at the back in summer. It serves an excellent range of cakes, including florentines, flapjacks and lovely meringues. Light lunches are served including soup, sandwiches and ploughman's and full meals are available. It is open every day from 9.30 am until 5 pm. Telephone: 01386 840386.

Starting point: Broad Campden (GR 158377).

How to get there: From the A44 Moreton-in-Marsh to Broadway road take the B4479 just west of Bourton-on-the-Hill, signed 'Blockley Village Centre'. In Blockley turn left, signed for the village centre, then right, signed 'Broad Campden'. At a T-junction after 2 miles, turn left. There is a broad verge where it is possible to park, 300 yards along on the left. Should this be full, there are other spots a little further on where a car can be left without causing inconvenience.

Map: OS Landranger 151 Stratford-upon-Avon.

Alternative starting point: If you want to visit the teashop at the beginning or end of the walk, start in Chipping Campden, where there is quite a lot of on-street parking. You would now commence at point 7.

The Walk

Broad Campden is an exceptionally attractive village with many delightful old houses, a pub, a Victorian chapel and an 18th-century Friends' Meeting House, passed at the end of the walk. It is centred on a curious raised green. For a time it was the home of Charles Ashbee, one of the many figures in the Arts and Crafts Movement who moved to the Cotswolds at the beginning of the 20th century. He was a socialist in the William Morris tradition who tried to oppose work that made people into appendages of machines, and he brought his group of craftsmen to Chipping Campden in 1902.

1. From the broad verge mentioned above, continue along the road. When the road bends left by the raised village green take a lane on the right and immediately turn right along another lane, signed 'unsuitable for motors'.

2. After 300 yards turn left along a public footpath, signed on a stone

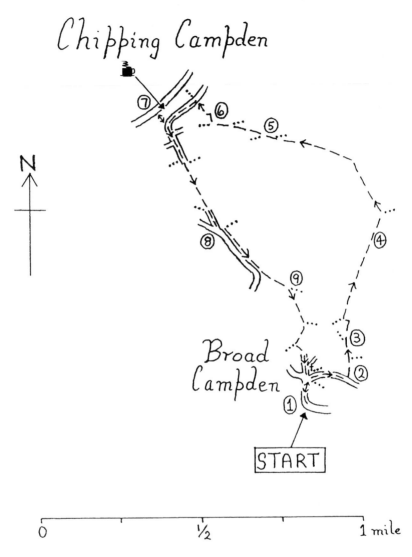

Chipping Campden

N

Broad Campden

①

START

0   ½   1 mile

slab. Go through the gate ahead which, at the time of writing, has a sign asking you not to let the goats escape and the gate appears to be goat proof. Immediately after a second gate bear left downhill with a wire fence on the left.

74

3. After 100 yards the path forks again. Bear right over a stile and continue along the left-hand side of a field for a further 100 yards to a double stile over the fences on the left. Immediately over the stiles turn right and walk along the right-hand side of the field to the far end, thus continuing in the same direction.

4. Continue across the middle of the next field and at the end bear half-left, slightly uphill, towards a small copse. Over a stile, bear half-left again just to the right of two isolated trees and continue in the same direction to the nearest of two stiles.

From this point there is a magnificent view across the fields to the church of St James in Chipping Campden. This is not actually passed on the route though you would certainly want to stretch any stroll round the town to include it. It took 50 years to build, starting in 1450, and is widely considered to be the finest of the magnificent Cotswold 'wool' churches, monuments to the prosperity and piety of the wealthy wool merchants. Inside is a treasure house of monuments and tokens of the town's long and rich history. There is a striking memorial brass to William Grevel, whose money helped build the church, and the monstrously grand marble tomb of Sir Baptist Hicks, later Lord Campden. He was so wealthy he could lend money to James I and half the court and he was a great benefactor of Chipping Campden, being responsible for the covered Market Hall and the almshouses near the church. His mansion next to the church was burned down by Royalist troops in the Civil War. It was later claimed that this was done to prevent it falling in enemy hands but it is more likely it was set alight by drunken soldiers raiding the cellars before fleeing. Now only two small lodges and a gatehouse remain.

5. Cross to a metal field gate and continue to a stile in the far right corner. Over the stile, head across the field and then turn left to walk by the stream. Do not cross the bridge but continue by the stream to a small gate.

6. Turn right through the gate and follow the path round to a track. Turn right and then left along a lane. When the lane bends left turn right on a signed bridleway through the Noel Arms car park to the main road. The teashop is 50 yards to the right.

Chipping is an old word meaning market and Campden had a market from the 13th century. It became the most important wool centre in the north Cotswolds, drawing traders from all over Europe. Its long and winding High Street has every sort of building from the 14th to 20th centuries. There is a glorious confusion of architectural features – triangular gables, mullioned and transomed windows, shielded by drip moulds and tall chimneys – but the whole is given a unity by the lovely golden stone of which the town is built.

Chipping Campden's prosperity declined with the wool trade in the 18th and 19th centuries. In 1902 it received an influx of new blood when Charles Ashbee moved his Guild of Craftsmen, 50 families, from the East End of London to the town. This was a brave endeavour, full of idealism, but it did not survive the realities of the economic depression, the First World War and mutual suspicion between the newcomers and the natives. However, this migration led to the formation of the Campden Trust in 1929 by artists and craftsmen including Norman Jewson and F. L. Griggs and this has done much to conserve the town as we see it today.

7. After tea and exploring Chipping Campden, return to the lane through the Noel Arms car park and turn right. The lane soon narrows to a path, leaving the town and reaching another road.

8. At the junction with the road turn left on a track and then immediately right on a path parallel with the road and thus continue in the same direction. When the hedge on the right ends bear slightly left on a clear path across a field.

9. At a signpost where the path forks bear right. At the end of the field go through a wooden kissing-gate and follow the signed path through the grounds of a house and then between buildings to a lane. Follow this into Broad Campden, passing the Friends' Meeting House, back to the start.

16

BOURTON-ON-THE-HILL and BATSFORD ARBORETUM

You could easily complete this walk in a short afternoon as, despite the extensive views, it is very easy. It uses clear paths that are simple to follow and there is very little climbing. However, it passes Batsford Arboretum, one of the showpiece sites of the Cotswolds with one of the finest private collections of rare trees and shrubs in Britain. A visit is particularly recommended in autumn when the colours are at their most glorious and time should be allowed for this. It is closed in the winter.
Distance: 4½ miles

The Apple Store teashop is in the garden centre at Batsford Arboretum, next to the entrance to the Arboretum itself. The building which houses it used to be the apple store for Batsford Manor and there is a wide terrace with tables overlooking the garden centre. It

serves an excellent range of home-made cakes and cream teas as well as light lunches, and is open every day from the beginning of March until the end of October between 10.30 am and 4.45 pm.
Telephone: 01386 700409.

When the teashop is closed an alternative source of refreshment is the flower-decked Horse and Groom in Bourton-on-the-Hill, passed just after the start of this walk.

Starting point: St Lawrence's church in Bourton-on-the-Hill (GR 175325).

How to get there: Bourton-on-the-Hill is on the A44 between Moreton-in-Marsh and Broadway. There is no public car park but there are several spots in the small roads behind the church where it is possible to park without causing inconvenience.

Map: Landranger OS 151 Stratford-upon-Avon.

Alternative starting point: If you want to visit the teashop at the beginning or end of the walk, start at Batsford Arboretum, where there is a large car park. You would now commence at point 12, leaving the garden centre along the entrance drive.

The Walk

The hill at Bourton-on-the-Hill has been known to travellers for a long time. The road used to be part of the turnpiked 'Great Road' from London and Oxford to Worcester. Now it is the A44 and lorries labouring up the gradient do detract from the charms of this otherwise most attractive village with its tiers of stone cottages, each with its flower-filled garden. The ancient church, Norman in origin, is worth a look and has many interesting features. The Winchester Bushel and Peck are reminders of the days before metric measures were the rule. A law passed in 1587 said that each parish had to have such measures, based on the standard at Winchester, to be used in the settlement of disputes. The ones in St Lawrence's are dated 1816 and bear the name of the magistrate's clerk of the day.

1. Facing the church, turn right along the main road. Some 60 yards after the Horse and Groom on the left, turn right along a public bridleway.

2. Turn left along a farm track. Turn right through the second field gate

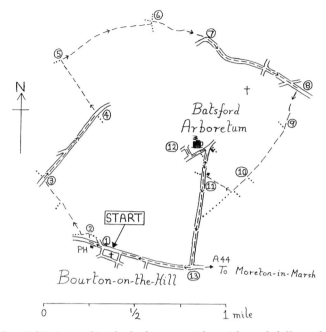

on the right, immediately before a cattle grid, and follow the fenced and hedged track to a lane.

3. Turn right for about ¹/₂ mile.

4. Immediately after the wall on the right becomes much higher, after a track on the right, turn left on a track. After 50 yards go through the right-hand one of two gates and follow the path down the left-hand side of two fields.

5. Turn right on a cross-path and follow it as it contours round the hillside for about ¹/₂ mile to end at a small gate.

This delightful path, lined with mature trees, overlooks the steep valley of Knee Brook. The village below is Blockley, whose early prosperity was based on sheep and wool, like so many Cotswold towns, with mills powered by the stream. The poverty that afflicted so many other towns and villages when the wool industry declined in the early 18th century was alleviated in Blockley when it turned to silk spinning for the Coventry ribbon weavers and at one time well over 500 people were employed in its six mills. In 1887 one of the old mills was used to generate electricity and Blockley claims to have been the first

English village to have electric lighting.

6. Bear left to a field gate. Do not go through it but turn right to walk along the left-hand side of a field. Some 50 yards after entering a second field bear right across the field to a gate onto a lane.

7. Turn left. At the crossroads continue in the same direction, signed 'Moreton-in-the-Marsh $1^1/2$', and carry on over a second crossroads.

8. About 100 yards after the second crossroads take a fenced path on the right. After a stile across the path, almost immediately cross a stile on the left onto a path along the right-hand side of a field.

9. At the end of the field cross a stile on the right and continue in the same direction to join a track. Continue along the track, passing the Victorian neoclassical Batsford Manor, which is not open to the public.

10. When the track bends sharply left continue ahead along the right-hand side of a field. At the end of the field cross a small bridge and go through a narrow belt of trees to a cross-path. Turn right and then bear to the left of a house to a drive.

11. Turn right and follow the signs to the garden centre. The teashop is in the far right corner of the garden centre and the entrance to the Arboretum is next to it. Tickets for the Arboretum may be bought in the garden centre.

There are over 1,500 species of trees and shrubs planted in the Arboretum on 50 acres of gently sloping hillside above the Evenlode valley. It was created in the 1880s by Bertie Mitford, the first Lord Redesdale, grandfather of the Mitford sisters (see walk 10). He had been a diplomat who spent much of his career in China and Japan and he imported many Oriental ideas as well as statues and plants. The Arboretum is open every day from Good Friday to the end of October or early November, depending when the autumn colours reach their peak, from 10 am to 5 pm (telephone: 01386 700409).

12. After tea retrace your steps and continue along the drive to the main road.

13. Turn right and follow the road through Bourton-on-the-Hill back to the start.

On the left at the entrance to the village you pass the elegant 18th-century Bourton House, whose gardens are open to the public on Thursday and Friday from the end of May to the end of September.

80

17

HIDCOTE and KIFTSGATE

This could be called the garden walk. It is a charming stroll on the Cotswold Edge and it therefore has some excellent views. An absolute must for anyone interested in gardens, it passes two outstanding examples, Hidcote Manor and Kiftsgate, taking tea at Hidcote. Garden enthusiasts will want to allow plenty of time to visit one or both gardens, perhaps making this an exceptionally interesting, all day expedition.
Distance: 3 miles.

At Hidcote Manor, owned by the National Trust, there are two places to have tea. Just off the car park, at the plant centre, is the tea bar. This is open between 10.30 am and 5.30 pm every day except Tuesday and Friday, from the beginning of April until the end of September. It serves cups of tea and an excellent range of cakes and sandwiches and there are tables around a cloister-like courtyard. The

restaurant is inside the garden, for which there is an entrance charge when the garden is open unless you are a member of the National Trust. It is more formal and has no outside tables. It serves full teas, including cream teas with clotted cream, and the same delicious range of cakes as well as full lunches. It is open from the beginning of April until the end of October and on some weekends in November and December, between 11 am and 5 pm.
Telephone: Tel: 01386 438703.

Teas are also available at Kiftsgate Manor in high season between Spring bank holiday Monday and August bank holiday Monday. Alternative possibilities when the tearooms at the gardens are closed are Myrtle's Tea Shop and the Three Ways Hotel in Mickleton, both very close to the start.

Starting point: Mickleton Memorial Fountain at the junction of the B4632 and the minor road to Broad Marston and Pebworth (GR 161436).

How to get there: The walk starts at Mickleton which is on the B4632 Stratford-upon-Avon to Broadway road. There are several spots around the village where you can park without causing inconvenience.

Map: OS Landranger 151 Stratford-upon-Avon.

Alternative starting point: If you want to visit the teashop at the beginning or end of the walk, start at Hidcote where there is a National Trust car park. You would now commence at point 9, following the lane towards Kiftsgate from the car park.

The Walk

The Victorian Memorial Fountain is an unusually restrained design by William Burges, a well-known exponent of High Victorian Gothic.

1. Walk along the B4632 towards Broadway. After 100 yards turn left at a phone box, soon passing the church on the left.

2. Continue along the surfaced track and 20 yards after passing the entrance to Field House take a path on the right to a gate. Follow this path along the right-hand side of a field to a gate into a strip of wood. On leaving the wood, continue in the same direction along the left-hand side of a field to a gate in the top left corner.

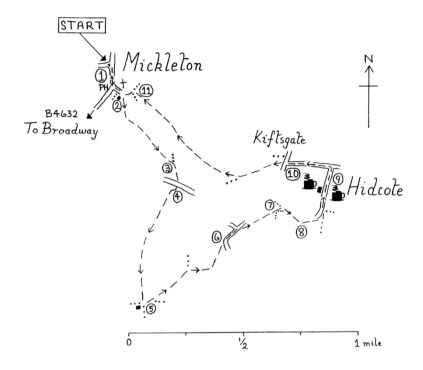

3. Through the gate bear half-right to the top corner of the field and a gate onto a lane. Take a path directly opposite, up some steps to a stile.

4. Turn right round the right-hand edge of a field and then follow the path into a wood. When the path leaves the wood, continue along the left-hand side of a field to a barn.

5. Turn left on a track and after 20 yards turn left again on a surfaced track. Continue along this to a T-junction with a road, bearing right at a cattle grid.

6. Turn left for about 100 yards. Just after a road on the left cross a stile on the right and walk diagonally across a field to a gate.

7. Bear left to an elaborate stile into a small enclosure and cross a second stile out of it. The path is not visible on the ground but bears half-right through some apple trees to a stile at the top right corner.

🥾 8. Over the stile turn left. At a cross-path turn left again. At a lane continue in the same direction through the hamlet of Hidcote Bartrim to the entrance to Hidcote Manor. The tea bar is on the right and the entrance to the gardens on the left.

Hidcote Manor Garden is of great comfort and no small interest to the ordinary gardener with a small plot to care for. It is inspiring to us all to realise that this magnificent place was established only in the 20th century on an open and windswept Cotswold hillside. When its creator, Major Lawrence Johnston, came to Hidcote in 1905 there was just the manor house, one cedar tree and a clump of beeches. It is not one garden on a huge scale but a series of interlinked areas, separated by hedges. These small gardens are each of a more domestic size and so are a stimulating source of ideas for the average gardener.

9. After tea and exploring the gardens return to the lane and continue along it, following round to the left at the car park entrance.

Kiftsgate Court Garden is perhaps not as well known as its famous neighbour but it should not be missed. It was created at about the same time as Hidcote by Mrs Heather Muir and it has continued to evolve under the guidance of her daughter and granddaughter. Situated on the edge of the scarp, it has winding paths leading down to a swimming pool on a grassy terrace with views across the Vale of Evesham. There is a notable collection of old roses, with the splendid Kiftsgate rose climbing to over 60 ft.

Kiftsgate is open from the beginning of April until the end of September on Wednesday, Thursday and Sunday between 2 pm and 6 pm. It is also open on bank holiday Mondays and Saturdays in June and July for the same hours (telephone: 01386 438777).

10. At the T-junction go straight across to a gate in the wall. The main entrance to Kiftsgate garden is 20 yards to the right. Follow the path downhill, with a particularly charming view ahead. After a gateway keep slightly right, more or less on the level, and when Mickleton church comes into view, head towards it to an awkward stile by a metal post. At this point in the walk there are many sheep tracks which are much clearer on the ground than the human tracks. Do not be misled by them as they head off in the wrong direction to nowhere in particular. After the stile the path is much more obvious.

11. Just before the churchyard turn left on a cross-path to a gate and follow the track past the church and back to the start.

18

THE ROLLRIGHT STONES

High on a ridge above Long Compton is one of the Cotswolds' most significant Bronze Age sites, now steeped in myth and legend. The Rollright Stones are on a quiet lane which follows the line of an ancient trading route along the ridge and this walk has extensive views, especially in winter when the trees are bare. After visiting the Stones it drops off the ridge to the picture postcard village of Little Rollright. The route then makes its way by quiet field paths almost to Great Rollright for tea before returning along the lane on the ridge to the start.
Distance: 4 miles.

Wyatts Tea Room differs from most of the teashops in this book because it is in a modern building – rather barn-like from the outside but very attractive inside with lots of pine and paintings by local artists. Outside there is a terrace with a splendid

view. It is attached to a farm shop which sells cakes and cheeses as well as fruit and vegetables. The teashop serves a delicious selection of cakes, sweets and cream teas with a variety of teas. For a light lunch, soup, salads and jacket potatoes are offered and there is a roast on Sunday. Open between 10 am and 6 pm every day.
Telephone: 01608 684835.

Starting point: At the junction of the A3400 and the minor road to Great Rollright (GR 306312).

How to get there: From the A3400 Stratford-upon-Avon to Chipping Norton road (which used to be the A34) 1^1/$_2$ miles south of Long Compton look for an offset crossroads with minor roads to Great and Little Rollright. Turn on the minor road to Great Rollright and immediately turn right into a small pull off by the junction. Note: there is a very similar crossroads 1^1/$_2$ miles further south of Long Compton towards Woodstock (GR 322296). Please be careful not to mistake this for the starting point.

Map: OS Landranger 151 Stratford-upon-Avon.

Alternative starting point: If you want to visit the teashop at the beginning or end of the walk, start at the teashop itself, where there is a car park. You would then commence the walk at point 10.

The Walk

The village nestling in the valley below is Long Compton. It was once said that it had enough witches to pull a cart up Long Compton Hill. In 1875 Ann Tennent, aged 79, was killed by a farmhand with a pitchfork because he thought she was a witch.

1. Return to the main road and take the lane opposite, signed for Little Rollright and Little Compton. Follow this as far as the Rollright Stones. The first group of stones, the Whispering Knights, is on the left through a field gate. The path leading to them is not a public right of way. The next, the King's Stone, is on the right opposite a layby and the main circle is a few yards further on, on the same side as the layby. A small charge is made for visiting the main circle.

The Rollright Stones are a collection of three separate groups – a circle of corroded, supposedly uncountable stones called the King's Men, a group of five a little distance away called the Whispering Knights, plotting the downfall

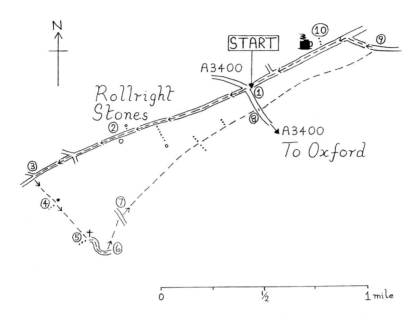

N

Rollright
Stones

START

A3400

A3400
To Oxford

0   ½   1 mile

of the King, and a large monolith across the road called the King's Stone.

The stones are steeped in myth and legend. Apparently an ancient chieftain, for example, was set on the conquest of all England. He was confronted here by a witch who spoke thus:

> *'If Long Compton thou canst see*
> *King of England thou shalt be.'*

As the chieftain stepped forward to survey his future conquests, Long Compton was hidden by the lie of the land and so the witch continued:

> *'As Long Compton thou canst not see*
> *King of England thou shalst not be.*
> *Rise up stick and stand still stone*
> *For King of England thou shall be none.*
> *Thou and thy men hoar stones shall be*
> *And I shall be an eldern tree.'*

In fact, the stones date from the Early Bronze Age, about 2000 BC, and may have served as a calendar. A line from the centre of the circle through the

King's Stone points to the star Capella at the spring equinox, the time to sow.

2. After visiting the stones, return to the lane and continue along it over a crossroads.

3. Opposite a road on the right turn left through a metal gate and follow a broad track downhill.

4. When the track turns sharp right by some barns on the left, continue in the same direction through a gap in the hedge and across the middle of a field towards Little Rollright church, making a perfect picture below.

5. Turn left on a track past the church. This soon becomes a lane through the hamlet.

6. Just after the lane bends left take a signed footpath on the left up the left-hand side of a field. When the hedge on the left ends continue ahead in the same direction across the field to a lane.

7. Cross the lane and continue on the waymarked path through five fields. At the end of the fifth field bear left through a belt of trees to the A3400.

At the end of the second field the Whispering Knights can be seen again. According to legend these were a group of knights who were plotting against the King when the witch struck. In fact, they are the collapsed remains of a Bronze Age burial chamber.

8. Turn right for 20 yards and then go up some steps on the left. At the top follow a signed path across a field and then go ahead with a hedge on the left to a lane.

9. Turn left and then left again at a road junction. The teashop is 200 yards ahead on the right.

This lane follows the line of an ancient trading route archaeologists have called the Jurassic Way. It ran from the mouth of the Humber to Salisbury Plain and the coast beyond. Some of it persists as part of the modern road network, as here, and it was much used by medieval traders taking wool to Bristol for export. The name Jurassic refers to the geological period when much of the rock beneath was laid down.

10. After tea continue along the lane back to the start.

19

HEYTHROP

This walk explores the eastern fringes of the Oxfordshire Cotswolds. It starts in the ancient village of Heythrop, notable for having two churches. Although the longest route in this book, much of it is on lanes and tracks and is easy going. You will walk through the grounds of Heythrop Park and along the banks of a tributary of the river Glyme. You may also see something most unusual in the English countryside...
Distance: 7 miles.

The teashop that is the focus of this walk is in The Quiet Woman Antique Centre so as well as enjoying tea, you can spend a pleasant hour rummaging around. The Quiet Woman was formerly a pub and there are various stories about the origin of the name. One is that one publican had a mute wife. A more romantic version is that

another inn-keeper's wife could be relied on to keep quiet about the activities of the highwaymen who hid out there. The excellent small teashop is most attractive, with fresh flowers on every table even during the winter. They serve a selection of sandwiches and cakes, with soup, paté, potted shrimps or delicious bacon rolls for lunch. They are open every day throughout the year until 5 pm, except Sunday when they close at 4 pm.
Telephone: 01608 646262.

Starting point: Heythrop village near the church (GR 351277).

How to get there: From the roundabout at the junction of the A44, A3400 and A361 a mile north-east of Chipping Norton take the A44 south for a quarter of a mile to a minor road on the left, signed 'Heythrop 2'. Drive along the lane to the village and park on the road by the church, where there is a wide verge.

Map: OS Explorer 191 Banbury, Bicester and Chipping Norton.

Alternative starting point: If you wish to start the walk at the teashop, it is on the A44 a mile west of Chipping Norton. There is a large car park but permission should be sought before leaving a car for a long period. You will then start the walk at point 11.

The Walk

The church you can see was built at the end of the 19th century. Beyond it is a much older one, dating from the 12th century. To visit it, go down the track to the modern church and through a small gate into the field next to the church. Walk alongside a ha-ha to an arched gate into the churchyard. When the new church was built, the old one was kept as a mortuary chapel. The enormous, ancient yew by the church is estimated to be 1,500 years old and so pre-dates any building on the site. In 1738, when Heythrop residents seemed reluctant to go to church, the incumbent refused to do morning services as the congregation consisted of just two old women who were never there at the same time. He complained that, 'to read to the church walls ... is to me a melancholy consideration'.

1. Continue along the lane, shortly passing a phone box on the right. Follow the lane down into a valley and up the other side to a T-junction.

2. Turn right, signed 'Enstone 3', for a good mile,

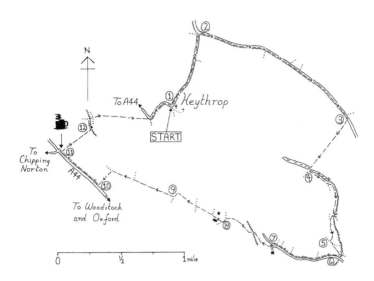

3. Some 75 yards after the entrance to Little Tew Grounds Farm on the left, turn right along a footpath along a surfaced drive.

Either side of the path are the winter quarters of a circus so you might be as startled as I was to find a giraffe or zebra looking over a gate.

4. At the end of a bridge turn left on an unsigned path to walk with the river on the left. Shortly after the first waterfall, when the path appears to bear right away from the river, bear left to walk next to the river, dotted with water lilies. Continue to the right of a wooden folly with a mossy roof to join a path coming in from the right.

The Talbot family, the Earls of Shrewsbury, bought the Manor of Heythrop at the end of the 17th century. At that time the Manor House was in the village but the Earl's Italian wife wanted a larger and more imposing home so the architect Thomas Archer was commissioned to build a new Hall in the Roman style. He was also responsible for landscaping the river into lakes and waterfalls and building the various follies the route passes. Archer was a student of Vanbrugh who was building Blenheim at much the same time (see walk 20) and there was considerable local rivalry. The Earl described Blenheim as 'a quarry above the ground'. The house was gutted by fire in 1831 and stood empty for 40 years. A railway millionaire, Albert Brassey, restored it. In 1920 the Hall became a Jesuit college then, in 1968, a conference and training centre, which it still is today.

5. At a T-junction with a cross path turn left. After 50 yards do not follow the obvious path ahead but go through a gap in the hedge on the right into a garage area. Immediately turn left, downhill. Continue past a metal footbridge on the left to reach a wide, surfaced drive.

6. Turn right for about half a mile.

7. At a building on the left, Talbot Hall, turn left along the drive to the Hall for 15 yards. Turn right on a signed public footpath, shortly passing two more follies, stone this time, and joining a path coming in from the left. Follow the signed bridleway from small gate to small gate. In a large field it is less obvious but if you bear left you will find another small gate. Go through this to emerge on a drive at a fork.

8. Turn left along the drive for 90 yards then turn right on a surfaced track, passing farm buildings on the left and a house on the right. Continue in the same direction on an unsurfaced track when the surfaced one bends right.

9. Some 60 yards after a sharp left-hand bend turn right along a similar track. Walk along it for half a mile then follow the main track round to the left to reach the main road.

10. Turn right for a good quarter of a mile to find the teashop on the right just after the traffic lights on the road to Chipping Norton.

11. Return to the road and turn left then immediately left again on a signed path.

12. At the bottom of a hill turn left on a path signed by a way-mark on a post, passing to the left of a house. Go through a gate on the right, over a stream and up through a wood, crossing a path. At the top of the hill go over a stile into a field. Press on along the left hand side of two fields and across a third to reach a lane. Turn right back to the start.

Albert Brassey was an energetic and philanthropic squire. The local houses were rebuilt in 1870 and apparently all his tenants were required to have the same curtains. He also built the modern church and a school for 150 children. However, his employee's children were not allowed to sit for scholarships because that would take them away from the estate. By 1963 there were only twelve children on the register and the school closed the following year.

20

BLENHEIM PARK and WOODSTOCK

This is an interesting and easy walk almost entirely on public footpaths in the park of Blenheim Palace. The walk leaves the park to visit the ancient town of Woodstock for tea.
Distance: 5 miles.

Harriets on the High Street in Woodstock is open every day throughout the year between 8.30 am (10 am on Sundays) and 5 pm (5.30 pm at weekends). It is a superb traditional teashop giving friendly and efficient service. The house is one of the oldest in Woodstock, dating from 1627, and is a most pleasant place to linger. There is an excellent range of cakes and other tea-time temptations including a clotted cream tea. For lunch, soup and sandwiches or pasties and quiche are served. A wide range of teas and coffees is offered or you can indulge in hot chocolate with whipped cream.

Telephone: 01993 811231.

Starting point: The layby by Blenheim's back gate (GR 425157).

How to get there: From the A4095 Bicester to Witney road 3 miles west of its junction with the A44 take a minor road signed 'Combe 1½ Stonesfield 3'. After passing under the railway continue ahead towards Combe and East End. After a further mile turn right on a road called East End and signed 'No Through Road'. Park in the large layby on the left.

Map: OS Landranger 164 Oxford.

Alternative starting point: If you want to visit the teashop at the beginning or end of the walk, start in Woodstock, where there is ample parking in the town car park, a few yards from the town centre down Hensington Road. To find the teashop return to the main road and cross over to the High Street. The tea shop is on the left. You will now start the walk at point 11. When you reach the main road turn left as far as a signed bridleway on the left leading through large green gates with the number 95 on them. Go through a second set of gates into the park and then turn right to reach a fork in the path by a house.

The Walk

1. Return to the road junction and continue in the same direction, passing Manor Farm (the second building on the left).

2. About 100 yards after Manor Farm take a public footpath on the right. Bear slightly left and then walk along the right-hand side of a hedge which starts partway up the field.

3. At the end of the field turn left and walk by the wall on the right for 80 yards. Cross the wall at a stile. Turn left on a track for 15 yards and then bear right. Follow this round to a cross-path in a wide clearing. Turn left for 40 yards and then bear right back into the wood. This is signed but is not obvious so needs to be looked for.

Some 2,100 acres of parkland surround Blenheim Palace. It was originally carved from the surrounding Wychwood Forest in the 12th century by Henry I who also built a hunting lodge nearby. This was enlarged into a palace by subsequent monarchs but during the 17th century it fell into ruin. In 1704 it was given to John Churchill, Duke of Marlborough, by a grateful nation in

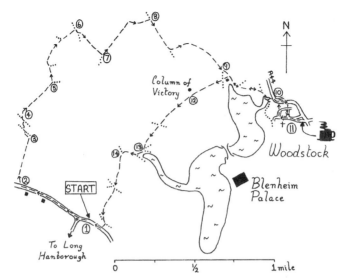

recognition of his success at the battle of Blenheim. The garden was designed by Capability Brown some half a century after the building of the palace and is often considered his masterpiece.

4. As the path leaves the wood, turn left and follow the path, initially along the left-hand side of the field and then continue ahead across the field to reach a track.

5. Turn left.

6. At a T-junction with a cross-track turn right. Follow this through a belt of pine trees then go over a stile on the left and cross to a second stile. The path is not visible on the ground but bears half right to a third stile.

7. Over the stile, turn left. The path lies to the left of a clump of trees, gradually diverging from the fence eventually to reach a stile in the far right-hand corner of the field. Over the stile, bear right to a gap in a fence surrounding a line of trees, seen ahead.

8. Turn right on a surfaced drive which is in line with the Column of Victory and the palace. Follow this as it bends left and right and goes down into a small valley.

This walk does not actually visit the palace and pleasure gardens but the route can be easily extended to include them (entrance charge). The palace is one of the grandest in England, with a magnificent series of staterooms full of outstanding tapestries, furniture and paintings. Winston Churchill was born here in 1874 and this is commemorated in an exhibition of memorabilia centred on the room where his mother actually gave birth. Blenheim is open daily from 10.30 am until 5.30 pm from mid-March until the end of October (telephone: 01993 811325).

9. When the drive forks (*) bear left along the top of the lake until the path approaches a wall and large gate on the left. The path ahead is not the public right of way and leads to the palace, gardens and various displays and tourist attractions. A charge is payable at the main Woodstock gate for these.

10. The right of way leads through the gate. It is unsigned from this side and leads to another gate onto the road. Turn right and follow the road to Woodstock. Half way up the hill turn right up the second set of steps. At the top follow Brown's Lane ahead into Woodstock. Cross to the far side of the Market Square to the Bear Hotel and turn left to the teashop on the right.

11. Turn left out of the teashop and walk almost to the end of the road. Turn right along Chaucer's Lane. When the lane bends right and becomes Harrison's Lane go ahead down some steps back to the main road. Turn left and retrace your steps almost to the fork indicated (*) above. Just before the fork, bear left in front of a house, then across a surfaced drive and continue in the same line uphill on the other side. The path is not visible on the ground but lies just to the left of an unfenced clump of trees and then to the left of the Column.

The Column of Victory offers a particularly fine view of the palace.

12. Continue past the column in the same direction to a fence corner and then walk ahead, with the fence on the right. When the fence ends go on in the same direction and cross a surfaced drive. Take the path opposite, now clearly visible, downhill.

13. Turn right at a T-junction with a cross-path to a stile over a wooden fence. Cross this and turn right to follow a grassy path to a surfaced drive.

14. Turn left and continue on this drive, ignoring all paths, to a drive junction. Turn right along the drive to the gate to the park. At the lane turn right, back to the starting point.